5,50
UP

D0936375

POLITICS
IN THE BORDER STATES

A STUDY OF THE
PATTERNS OF POLITICAL ORGANIZATION,
AND POLITICAL CHANGE, COMMON TO THE BORDER
STATES — MARYLAND, WEST VIRGINIA, KENTUCKY AND MISSOURI.

John H. Fenton

THE HAUSER PRESS
Galleon books

Publishers   *Printers*

NEW ORLEANS, LA.

F
209
F4

Copyright, 1957

HAUSER PRINTING COMPANY, INC.
NEW ORLEANS, LA.

116587

PREFACE

THIS BOOK is concerned with four of the Border States: Missouri, Kentucky, West Virginia, and Maryland. These four were selected because they are contiguous and are typical of the Border State region. In terms of political behavior, the Border States are interesting for their own sakes, resting as they do between North and South and thus providing something of a battleground where the two cultures vie for supremacy. However, the political patterns of the Border States are assuming a more universal significance as the South becomes more industrialized and thus takes on some of the cultural contradictions that heretofore were only to be found in the Border States. Consequently, the Border States have become an important indicator of what the future may hold in store for the South.

A central purpose of this study has been to find patterns of political organization and political change that are common to the Border States and that, consequently, might have a certain universality, at least within the political environment of the United States. In some ways the Border State environment is unique. However, many of the problems of the Border State politicians, in terms of such things as organization and relations with interest groups, and of the Border State

i

people, in terms of such things as farm prices and wage levels, are far from unique.

Within the hackneyed confines of a preface it is difficult, indeed, to convey the sense of gratitude I feel to so very many people for their aid and advice. It is impossible to name the more than one hundred political, labor, farm, and business leaders with whom I discussed the politics of their respective states. The vast majority of them were incredibly generous with their time and knowledge of the politics of their states.

The word "inspire" has become woefully weary from over-use. However, its meaning remains intact when applied to the counsel provided me by Professor V. O. Key, under whose guidance this study was originally undertaken at Harvard University as a doctoral dissertation. I must also extend my thanks to Professor Bennett Wall of the University of Kentucky for his aid in so many ways.

A Fellowship awarded me by the Social Science Research Council made possible my extended trips to the Border States. The execution of such an ambitious project would have been impossible without the generosity of the Council.

Finally, it is customary to salute one's spouse—and for some very excellent reasons. She typed most of the drafts, made excellent substantive suggestions, and at the same time cooked the meals and cared for our child.

— JOHN H. FENTON

TABLE OF CONTENTS

LIST OF TABLES

LIST OF ILLUSTRATIONS

LIST OF ILLUSTRATIONS—(Continued)

CHAPTER I

POPULATION AND POLITICS

IN THE SPRING and in the fall, when the cool air retreats to the north or when the warm air grudgingly withdraws to the south, the residents of the Missouri plains keep one eye upon the sky as they plant their corn or harvest their wheat. It is in this middle area of the nation that a funnel is most likely to dart out of the heavens and twist and skip its way across the countryside, leaving broken homes and bodies in its wake.

Geographically and culturally, as well as climatically, the Border States are middle states. It is along the northern fringes of the Border States that two great population fronts and cultures meet. One of these population fronts was born in the humid Tidewater region of Virginia, Maryland, and the Carolinas; and the other has its roots in the rockbound coasts of the states to the north. The meeting of these two population fronts along the northern reaches of the Border States created in the mid-nineteenth century a cultural condition analogous to the meeting of cold and warm masses of air.

During the decade following 1850, the farmers of Kansas and Missouri often paused anxiously in their work to scan the far horizons. Their eyes did not search for clouds of concern to meteorologists, but for billows of dust raised by the hoofs of horses ridden by Quantrill's raiders or by the avenging Jayhawkers, led by the "wild-eyed" John Brown, producing human

storms as the northern and southern migrations collided.

Table 1 tells arithmetically of the meeting of North
and South in the Border States and the character of
that meeting. Reference to the Table shows that most
of the people who had newly made their homes in the
Border States in 1850 were from the South or sister
Border States, but a substantial proportion of the newcomers (approximately 40 per cent) were from Northern states or were foreign born. After 1850, the flow

TABLE 1

PER CENT OF STATE'S POPULATION NON-NATIVE, AND
PER CENT OF NON-NATIVE POPULATION FROM
WHITE SOUTH OR BORDER STATES
1850-1950

	1850	1880	1900	1920	1940	1950
Kentucky						
% Non-Native	22	15	12	12	11	13
% of Non-Native from White South or Border State	59	33	33	33	27	23
Maryland [1]						
% Non-Native	19	18	20	24	29	37
% of Non-Native from White South or Border State	16	22	20	21	28	32
Missouri						
% Non-Native	53	42	35	30	27	28
% of Non-Native from White South or Border State	56	31	23	17	19	21
West Virginia						
% Non-Native	___[1]	36	20	24	20	19
% of Non-Native from White South or Border State	___[1]	61	35	33	35	32

[1] Maryland represents a special case because it was a seed bed for western
migration in 1850. No 1850 statistics are available for West Virginia, but figures
for Virginia would indicate that the distribution of population in West Viriginia
in 1850 was similar to that of Kentucky and Missouri.

of Southern white people into the Border States tended to decline but the flow of Northern population remained relatively constant or increased, thus resulting
in an increasing proportion of the new population
originating from Northern states.

The population movement into the Border States
created an essentially similar political and cultural
configuration in all four states. Tidewater Maryland
was settled at an early date by people from England
who harbored a desire to be the landed gentry of the
new world. A plantation system was adopted in the
Tidewater region and thousands of slaves were imported to work the land. By 1790, there were 103,000
slaves as opposed to 190,000 free people in the state
of Maryland. Most of the slaves were concentrated in
the Tidewater section of the state, where very nearly
a fifty-fifty division between free and slave folk existed.
In the western part of Maryland, however, many Germans and migrants from Pennsylvania were building
big barns and small homes in 1790, a practice foreign
to the state at that date, and harbingering basic
changes in the state's culture.

Before the turn of the nineteenth century there was
little or no uncultivated land remaining in Tidewater
Maryland. The sons and daughters of the Tidewater
Bourbons, eager to become land barons in their own
right, followed the trail marked by the feet of Boone
to the fertile Bluegrass of Kentucky and the Greenbrier Plateau region of West Virginia. In their turn,
the sons of the Bluegrass Bourbons left their homes
for the unclaimed land of the Little Dixie section of
Missouri. The Bourbons carried with them both their
slaves and customs wherever they went. They estab-

lished great plantations, built gracious homes, and became social, economic, and political leaders in the communities in which they resided. Politically, prior to the Civil War, the people of the Bourbon centers tended to cast the majority of their vote for the Whig party. Since the Civil War, the white vote of the plantation sections has been determinedly Democratic; but there has been evidence of a shift of the Bourbon vote to the Republican party since the New Deal, and particularly in 1952 and '56.

In concert with the settlement by the Bourbons of the more fertile bottom-lands of the Border States, a different sort of person built rude cabins in the mountains. To the Scotch immigrants, the mountains of North Carolina and Virginia looked like home, and to their sons and daughters the mountains of Tennessee and Kentucky, and the Ozarks of Missouri had the comfortable feeling of an armchair grown old in the service of its master. These mountain people were and are an isolated, independent, self-reliant type, and they react similarly to national issues, such as slavery and the New Deal. In the main, the highlanders of the Upper South were indifferent to slavery as an institution, but were strongly loyal to the Union. Following the Civil War the mountain folk tended to identify the Democratic party with rebellion, and became staunch supporters of the Republican faith. To them, as well as to their Bourbon opponents in the lowlands, elections after the Civil War were not sporting contests between essentially like-minded people, but an extension of the battles of Gettysburg and Shiloh, Chattanooga and Bull Run.

A last pre-Civil War group of considerable importance in the culture and politics of the Border States was the many small farmers, artisans, and shopkeepers who, at the time of the Civil War, had their roots in the South, and, though not important slave owners, sympathized with their mother culture in its conflict with the "Yankees." Many, probably most, of these people were Jacksonian Democrats before the Civil War, and found renewed reason in the trials of civil strife to remain loyal Democrats. More often than not the economic interests of the small farmer have been in conflict with those of the Bourbons. Before the Civil War this conflict of interests was resolved by interparty contests between Whigs and Democrats. Since 1865, the Bourbons and the small farmers have, in the main, been forced to resolve their differences within the folds of the Democratic big top, but with occasional defections to a third party or to the Republican party when factionalism has become over-heated.

After the Civil War the settlement pattern of the Border States underwent a dramatic change. As Table 1 shows, the proportion of non-natives to the total population declined precipitously, and most importantly, the decline in the proportionate size of the non-native population was largely due to the drying up of white Southern immigration into the Border States. As the table indicates, in every Border State but Maryland the relative size of the non-native white Southern population was cut by almost 50 per cent from 1850 to 1900.[1] Inevitably this change in the source of the Border States' population worked a

---

[1] After the Civil War, Maryland's non-native population tended to increase due to reverse migration from the west back to the east. In addition, the increase in the proportion in the non-native population from the South is due in large part to the movement of Washingtonians into suburban Maryland.

revolution in their political and cultural makeup.

Not surprisingly, most of the people entering the Border States from the North made their homes in the northern reaches of the Border States and in their cities and helped swell the Republican vote in these areas. German immigrants also entered the Border States during the mid-nineteenth century. The Germans had as their port of entry to the United States the city of Baltimore, and made their way inland via the waterways. By 1870, there were large German settlements in Baltimore city and surrounding counties; in Covington and Newport, Kentucky, across the Ohio River from Cincinnati; in Louisville, Kentucky; in St. Louis city and county and in the counties west of St. Louis along the south bank of the Missouri River (see Figure 1). The Germans were inclined Democratic before the Civil War, but because of their strong abolitionist sentiment and their aversion to the idea of a weak central government they tended to desert to the ranks of the Republican party after the Civil War.

The influx of propertyless immigrants, northerners, and Negroes into the Border States after the Civil War helped accelerate the growth of their cities. These lost and bewildered people were befriended by political leaders who were quick to recognize and lay claim to a lode of votes. The political leaders helped many of the immigrants find homes and jobs, and provided aid when they became enmeshed in the city's legal machinery. In return for favors of such monumental importance in the scale of values of these people, it seemed like small payment, indeed, to vote as the kindly politicians suggested.

By this time, the vote of the Border States, outside the principal cities, was very evenly and rigidly divided between the Republican and Democratic parties. Therefore, the development of a sizeable manipulable vote in the cities was a factor of no mean importance. Before 1932, the urban political leaders were the handmaidens of the business community. Consequently, the vote produced by this new urban population in crucial elections, such as 1896, was heavily weighted on the side of conservative candidates. The New Deal, however, by helping create large labor organizations introduced competition for this manipulable vote in many Border State cities.

The importance of the colored population in the cultural and political history of the Border States cannot be overstated. Before 1932, the colored vote, where cast, was unwaveringly Republican. Due in part to the Republican bias of the colored voters, the division between the two parties in sections such as the Maryland Tidewater and the Kentucky Bluegrass has been narrow since 1872. Since 1932, the colored vote in the cities has been captured by Democratic candidates, and in the rural areas the number of colored Democrats has increased markedly.

The fear of "Black Republican" rule was once a rallying pole around which both Populists and Bourbons could be united. In recent years, however, the political value of this issue has diminished. It is difficult to excite Border State whites about the Negro problem when so few colored people live there. The proportion of the total population which is colored has declined in the only two Border States in which it was ever substantial, i.e., Maryland and Kentucky.[1] Finally, it has become politically dangerous to antagonize the colored voters, because they have become issue conscious in their vote.

Missouri provides an excellent example of the effect of the population changes which have been described on the political makeup of the Border States. Figures 1, 2, and 3 demonstrate graphically the relationship between the composition of Missouri's population and its political bias. The state of Missouri is used in these figures because its relatively recent and rapid settlement makes possible the compilation of reliable data concerning the sources of its population.

The area colored black in Figure 1 was settled largely by people from Virginia and Kentucky, according to the *United States Census of 1870*. Missourians call the section north of the Missouri River where the Kentuckians and Virginians settled in great numbers "Little Dixie." It is the part of the state toward which the sons and grandsons of Tidewater and Bluegrass Bourbons were attracted. Figure 3 serves to demonstrate the Democratic proclivities of the residents of the section. The presidential elections of 1896 and 1904 are used in Figures 2 and 3 because they mark low tides in Republican and Democratic fortunes, respectively, in the state, and thus delineate areas of pronounced political strength. In the election of 1904 every county but two of the 31 largely settled by Kentuckians or Virginians voted Democratic.

Identified by dots in Figure 1 is a line of counties

---

[1] The 1950 percentage non-white population of the four states was as follows: Missouri, 8 per cent; Kentucky, 7 per cent; West Virginia, 6 per cent; and Maryland, 17 per cent.

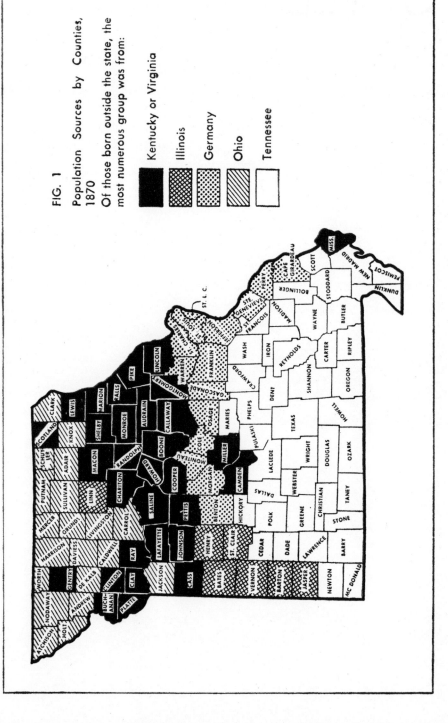

FIG. 1

Population Sources by Counties, 1870

Of those born outside the state, the most numerous group was from:

Kentucky or Virginia

Illinois

Germany

Ohio

Tennessee

running both south and west from St. Louis. It is in these counties that the German population was the dominant group in 1870. The "German belt" has since girdled the state as far as Lafayette county. Figure 2 demonstrates the Republican sympathies of the German population. In the 1896 election, eleven of the fifteen German counties voted Republican.

The counties in Figure 1 which are differentiated by black diagonal lines were settled, in large part, by people from Ohio. The land in this section of Missouri is fertile, and the barns, the homes, the people, and the Republican vote they cast are all more like unto the countryside south of Columbus, Ohio, than the magnolia-scented banks of the Potomac. Comparison of Figures 1, 2, and 3 shows the tendency of these Ohioans to vote Republican.

The Osage Plains section south of Kansas City, in Jackson county, was settled by people from Illinois. Despite the apparent Northern antecedents of the Osage Plains citizens, the section became a Democratic stronghold following the Civil War. The explanation for this anomaly has two parts. In the first place, it was this section of Missouri which suffered most from the border warfare between Quantrill's men and the Kansas Abolitionists. During the Civil War the Union commander of the district issued the notorious "Order Number 11." Very simply, the Order required that the residents of the area abandon their farms and homesteads and find shelter elsewhere. There ensued scenes which rivaled in terms of human suffering the tragic exodus of European cities during World War II. The bitterness engendered by this experience has been reflected in the vote of the section until relatively recently. Secondly, many of the settlers of the Osage Plains were from the Little Egypt section of southern Illinois; a section which was originally settled by Southerners, was rife with Copperheads during the Civil War, and is a Democratic stronghold in rural Illinois.

South of the Missouri River valley and west of the Mississippi valley, is a land of rugged mountains, broken by swift streams which form occasional oases of fertile bottom land. This section of Missouri was settled, primarily, by Tennesseans. Figures 2 and 3 show that the western portion of the Ozarks is inclined toward the Republican banner, whereas the eastern part is Democratic. C. O. Sauer in his article dealing with "Geography and the Gerrymander" explains the existence of a Democratic beach-head in the Republican Ozarks in terms of its settlement pattern. According to Sauer, the rocky crags of the eastern Ozarks were too rugged for even the hardy highlander. Consequently, most of the residents of the section are huddled in the fertile valleys. These valleys, it seems, were settled by Southern slave owners, whose progeny are still the dominant group in the valley communities.[1]

The political complexion of the Ozarks section can then be explained in the following terms. The western Ozarks were settled largely by hill people from eastern Tennessee and Kentucky. These people, like their kinfolk in Tennessee were pro-Union during the Civil War and were inclined toward the Republican banner thereafter. The eastern Ozarks, on the other hand, were settled in the main by lowlanders from Tennessee

---

[1] C. O. Sauer, "Geography and the Gerrymander," *American Political Science Review*, Vol. XII, 1918, pp. 410-11.

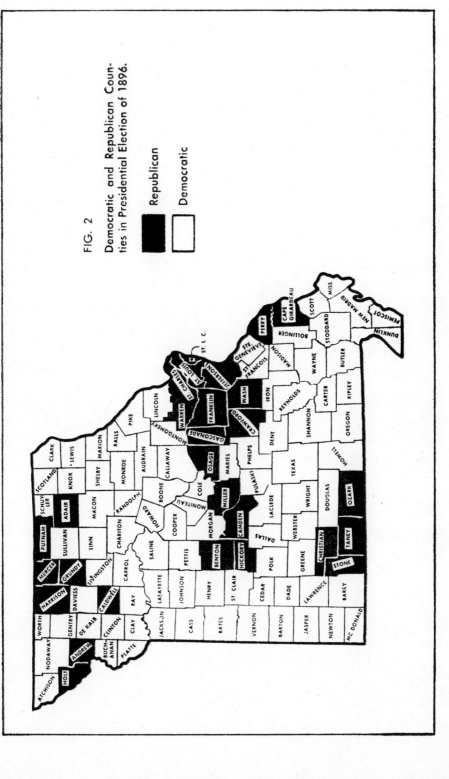

FIG. 2

Democratic and Republican Counties in Presidential Election of 1896.

Republican

Democratic

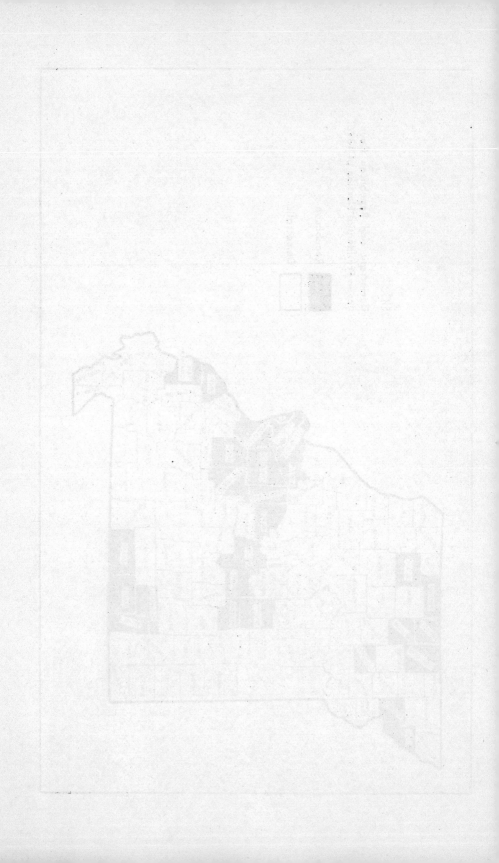

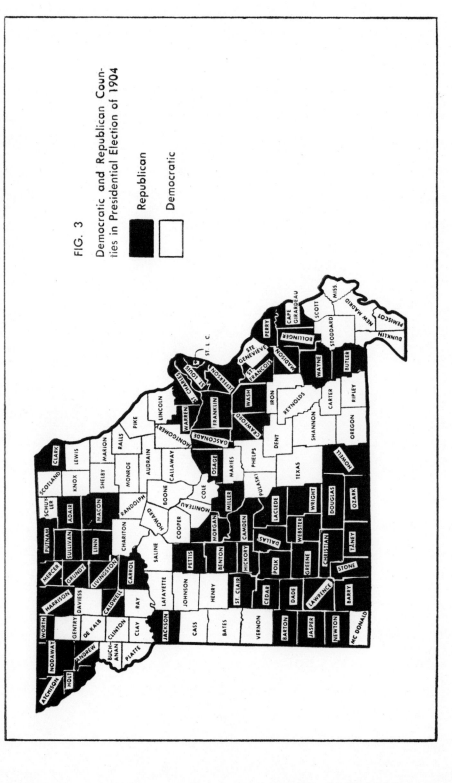

FIG. 3

Democratic and Republican Counties in Presidential Election of 1904

Republican

Democratic

and Kentucky whose sympathies were with the South during the Civil War and who have voted Democratic since.

The settlement pattern of Missouri is illustrative of all the Border States. They are neither North nor South, neither Bourbon nor Yankee, but partake of elements of both. Essentially, they are middle states.

Some of the political consequences of the type of culture pattern created by the Border States' unique population development are:

1. *A narrow numerical division between the two major political parties.*

The term "Border States" has reference to the narrow division between the Democratic and Republican parties as well as the geographic position of the states resting between North and South. The existence of two political parties of very nearly equal weight, numerically, is a direct effect of the physical location of the Border States. The settlers from the North and, before 1932, the Negroes, have been Republican adherents, whereas the population entering from the South has been dominantly Democratic. The result has been a rather narrow numerical division between the two parties, with the Democrats enjoying a slight advantage.

2. *A long run plus Republican trend.*

Many factors have entered into the long run plus Republican trend observable in all the Border States, interrupted in 1932, but continuing since that date. One of the dominant variables responsible has been the increasing proportion of the new Border State population that has emanated from the North. The election returns from the Border States have reflected this gradual accretion of Republican strength. In 1932, the New Deal, by capturing the vote of much of the laboring population, particularly in the coal mining areas, temporarily reversed the area's plus Republican trend. However, the more recent trend in all the Border States is back toward a pre-1932 division between the two parties.

3. *Chronic factionalism within the Democratic party.*

The Border States are frequently characterized in this study as Three-Party States. The severe intra-party strife which besets the Democratic party in the Border States inspires this characterization. Before the Civil War, the Border State Bourbons were, in the main, Whigs. The independent farmers and urban workers, on the other hand, were Democrats. Therefore, the conflict of economic interests between these groups was the issue of inter-party electoral contests. Following the Civil War both groups found themselves members of the Democratic party. Consequently, the struggle over "who shall rule" has had to be resolved within the ranks of the Democratic party. However, factional victory has never been decisive, because the Republican party stands ever ready to assume power if Democratic factionalism alienates a sufficient number of its partisans.

4. *A unique type of political organization.*

A species of political organization has evolved out of the Border State environment specifically designed to bridge the gap between the Democratic party's conservative or Bourbon and liberal factions. In Kentucky, the bridging medium is called the "Administration group" and in West Virginia the "Statehouse faction." In both states the organizational pattern is identical. The governor is a "strong" executive and thus controls the emoluments of power, such as patronage and the distribution of contracts. Due to their political power the governors of West Virginia and Kentucky are able to marshal political organizations relatively independent of the economic and social factions of the party. These purely political groupings within the Democratic party control the spoils of power. Through a Solomon-like division of spoils and the nomination of candidates acceptable to all factions of the party, a degree of party unity is maintained. It is because of the experience of uniting North and South which successful Border State politicians have enjoyed that they are so often found in positions of leadership in the Democratic party.

We turn now to a more detailed examination of the political consequences of the Border State culture. To some extent the Border State problems and the adjustments thereto are unique. However, the political problems of organization, factionalism, and change have a universality which should make the Border State experience interesting to residents of other states. Kentucky is the first state to be examined. Kentucky precedes the other Border States because its three-party structure is clean-cut and thus provides a model in terms of which the political structures of the other Border States take a readily recognizable shape.

CHAPTER II

KENTUCKY — A THREE-PARTY STATE

THE STRUGGLE for political power in Kentucky is a
many-sided affair. The center of the state's political stage is held by the periodic conflicts that take place
within the Democratic party between shifting coalitions of political leaders for control of that party.
These factional battles are decisive because nomination on the state's Democratic ticket has been virtually
tantamount to election since the Civil War. The Republican party, however, is strong enough to capitalize
on any defections in Democratic ranks which occur
as the result of intraparty rows. Therefore, the battle
between the two parties is also an important part of
the political picture in Kentucky, but is often only
another side of the struggle within the Democratic
party.

Immediately offstage, but no less important in Kentucky politics, are the people and organizations loosely
described as the "Interests." The Louisville and Nashville Railroad Company; the liquor, racetrack, coal,
and farm interests have oftentimes been the moving
figures behind the drama of Kentucky politics and
politicians. Kentuckians describe their state as conservative because of the success this particular category
of interest group has often enjoyed in nominating and
electing candidates of its choice, and in obtaining the
passage or defeat of measures affecting their interests.

Political organization is the environment within
which the postures of the principals of the political

drama take form. It is the stage and the setting. Therefore, an understanding of Kentucky's political battles pre-supposes a grasp of the nature of political organization in the state. The term "political organization" is probably the most used and abused term in the lexicon of politics. In the minds of many people the term provokes images of shadowy, sinister men who smoke cigars and collect shake-down money from the cop on the beat. A look at political organization in Kentucky soon dissipates this stereotype-barrier.

Political Organization in Kentucky

There are five broad classes of people who are active in day-to-day politics at the county level. These groups are: 1) the office holder, 2) the disappointed office seeker, 3) the merchant who is the recipient of contracts, 4) the disappointed merchant who seeks contracts, 5) the professional politician.

"Interest groups" are a sixth category of people who are active in politics at all levels of government. The activities and objectives of such groups are, however, generically different from those of the five other groups named. The office holder, contract recipient and the professional politician are almost wholly absorbed in the mechanics of winning elections. The election for these people is an end in and of itself. The Baptist minister or Catholic priest, the corporation president, the labor or farm leader, the reform leader, is, on the other hand, issue oriented. In general, these people share the sentiment voiced by a president of the Louisville and Nashville Railroad Company when he said, "Damn the Republicans. Damn the Democrats. We are not office holders, we are not office seekers."

An interest group may, on occasion, make use of a political organization to obtain the election or defeat of a candidate, but the objective is not the election of a person to an office, but, rather, opposition to or support of some issue. If an interest group enters into the hurly burly of politics through the creation of a political organization of its own, then it also partakes of one or more of the five categories of people who take a day-to-day interest in politics.

It is the professional politician and those who are interested in offices and contracts with whom this discussion is now concerned. The best manner in which to get acquainted with these people is to meet them as individuals. Three fairly typical Kentucky counties have been selected for this purpose.

1. *Nelson County*

Nelson county is located in the Bluegrass section of the state and is very near to being at the state's midpoint both geographically and culturally. On the western and southern borders of the county are the Knobs, forty miles to the north is Louisville, and immediately to the east is the Inner Bluegrass. "My Old Kentucky Home," memorialized by Stephen Foster according to popular legend, is at Bardstown, the county seat, where the manorial "Home of Three Governors" is also located. As though to leave no loose ends, the amber fluid in the Kentucky Colonel's mint julep is manufactured here. No fewer than eleven bourbon distilleries spill "the smell of prosperity" over the Nelson county countryside.

The county differs from the remainder of the state in that a majority of the population is of the Catholic faith. A Trappist monastery is to be found here, as well as a rather famous cathedral and several Catholic schools.

Politics is a matter of passionate concern to virtually everyone in Nelson county. Whether he be a farmer at Cox's Creek or a bank president in Bardstown, the average citizen is a violent partisan in every election. Like most of the Bluegrass, the county has been Democratic since the Civil War, but was Whig prior to that event.

Politically, the county was dominated by Ben Johnson and Dan Talbott, two prominent figures in Kentucky politics, from the turn of the century until their deaths in the early 1940's. Talbott was Johnson's junior partner, as well as son-in-law, until the twilight of their careers in the late thirties when they quarreled and went their separate ways.

An impressive percentage of the well-to-do people of the county thank Ben Johnson for their fine homes and prosperous businesses. It was these favored folk who received state contracts and state sinecures, while the Johnson-Talbott regime ruled. However, neither Johnson nor Talbott left fine homes or large sums of money. For them, the reward of the political game was political power.

Johnson's political weapon was double-bladed; on the one side was the edge of fear, and on the other the block portion of the Catholic vote. There are two precincts in Nelson county which can cast a near unanimous vote for almost any candidate of any party, depending upon the whims of its leaders. One of the precincts is the Trappist monastery and the other is

Nazareth Academy. Johnson had the ear of the shepherds who tended these two flocks and thus was in a position to swing several hundred votes in almost any direction.

Johnson used his power. It is said of him that "he would do almost anything for you if he liked you, but he would destroy you if he didn't." His power to destroy was great. It went beyond the power to confer or withhold contracts or jobs. It included one's ability to obtain credit at the bank, renewals on mortgages, business from Catholics or distillers. In short, his power was very nearly total.

Ben Johnson's death left a vacuum in the leadership of Nelson county's Democratic party that was not immediately filled. Instead of one political leader, many factions developed in the county. In 1955, the two most important political leaders in Nelson county were W. G. A. Sympson and Judge R. L. Beeler. Sympson was a garage owner, automobile dealer, mayor of the city of Bardstown and "Administration man" for the county. Judge Beeler was a professional politician. He was county road engineer for some twenty-five years before being elected to the post of county judge.

Judge Beeler's influence in the county was due to the county's generosity to the unfortunate. While county road engineer, he was always asked to deliver the shoes, blankets, food, coal and the like that the county distributes to its needy. The hungry and the cold who were brought succor by Judge Beeler thanked him and not the impersonal community for their relief. In addition, the Judge enjoyed the opportunity to exercise some discretion in the distribution of relief goods.

The gratitude of these people for what they deemed the Judge's humane interest in their well-being disposed them to accept without serious question his suggestions as to their behavior on election day. The Judge, however, never succeeded in extending his influence beyond the confines of the county and thus was unable to assume the position of "boss" of the county. For example, instead of naming Beeler as Administration man for the county in 1947, Governor Clements selected W. G. A. Sympson. Beeler was passed over, in all probability, because he was not "accepted" by the middle class of the community.

However, W. G. A. Sympson, the Administration man, and Judge Beeler worked closely together. In fact, the Judge was an Administration-backed candidate for election as county judge. However, Sympson and not Beeler had the ear of the governor relative to Nelson county matters.

The post of Administration man, held by Bill Sympson from 1947 to 1955, is nowhere to be found in the organization charts of the state government. It is not a post which is mentioned in the newspaper as one to which a person is appointed. It is an informal working relation between a local person and the governor. Nevertheless, it is, perhaps, the most important single political post in the county. In Kentucky, there is no necessary correspondence between lines of authority in the party and the identity of the Administration man. The person holding the position may or may not be the county chairman of the Democratic party. In some instances the Administration man is the county judge, the most important elective office in the county. In Nelson county, however, Bill Sympson held no elective or official party post at the time of his appointment.

Bill Sympson obtained the post of Administration man in a "standard" fashion. In 1947, Earle Clements, later United States Senator, was the Democratic candidate for governor. In the primary campaign Sympson offered his services to Clements as his Nelson county campaign manager. In both the primary and general election Sympson devoted prodigious efforts in Clements' behalf. Following Clements' inauguration as governor, Sympson was named Administration man for the county.

The authority and duties of the Administration man are broad. In the first place, he enjoys the confidence of the governor insofar as employment by the state of persons residing in the county is concerned. It is virtually impossible to obtain a position with the State Highway Department without his recommendation. Because the state employees feel obligated to the Administration man for their employment and dependent upon his good will for their continued connection to the Commonwealth's breast, they also feel an obligation to heed calls upon them to perform many tasks not directly related to highway work. For example, the state employees are expected to make generous election "contributions" and to place themselves at the disposal of the Administration man for campaign work. Any failure of a state employee to obey an Administration request would almost certainly result in his dismissal.

Succession to the august office of Nelson county

Administration man brings with it power that transcends the purely political sphere. This power can be used to help or hinder business compatriots in their pursuit of the Department of Finance's Grail. A word from the Administration man is often instrumental in securing a lucrative contract with the state for a fellow townsman. Similarly, he can deny state business to enemies.

The building and routing of highways is another area in which the Administration man enjoys considerable authority. If a group of people feels that a highway should be constructed from one point to another within the county they do not look to their State Representative or Senator for presentation of their demands, but go to the Administration man with their request. If he decides that the demand is righteous (and/or backed by a sufficient number of political guns), the road, in all probability, is built. If a group were so ill-advised as to bypass the Administration man by going straight to the state authorities with their demands, the first question asked by state officials would be, for example, "Have you talked this over with Bill Sympson?," followed by the suggestion that he be consulted.

In addition, the Administration man can be most helpful to favored citizens with reference to the routing of highways. If a front yard were about to be lost or a farm or community by-passed because of the "ill-considered" decision of highway engineers, then the Administration man can often be prevailed upon to arrange relocation of the highway. Hair-raising turns on Kentucky highways often testify to the good offices of Administration men.

In Nelson county, because Bill Sympson was Administration man and thus enjoyed the attendant political power, he was also mayor of Bardstown. And because he was both mayor of Bardstown and Administration man, both the city and state police made use of Sympson's garage whenever feasible. In addition, when vehicles were purchased by the state, he was likely to receive an important part of the state's business.

Sympson's ability to reward and punish provided him with much power, but also earned him a good deal of enmity. The garage owners without state business were unhappy; defeated candidates and their supporters, disgruntled and bitter, decried "dictation" by the Administration crowd. Finally, the county judge was primarily a county courthouse man and was not a creature of the Administration. Therefore, the structure of power built by Sympson was strong but brittle.

The Democratic gubernatorial primary of 1955 brought to an end Sympson's hold on political influence, wealth and power in the community. In that primary, "Happy" Chandler was the successful anti-Administration candidate. One of Chandler's first acts in the campaign was the development of an organization in each county of the state. In Nelson county the person who requested and was awarded the job as "Happy's" campaign manager was Frank Wilson, a rival garage owner and automobile dealer. Therefore, the loss of the primary by the Administration resulted in the displacement of Sympson by the rival garage owner as Administration man, and the transfer to Wilson of all the privileges and emoluments appertaining thereto.

2. Harlan County, "Whiskey, Wedlock, and Workers"

"Bloody" Harlan is located in the heart of Kentucky's Eastern Coal section. The county was steadfastly Whig before the Civil War and remained equally devoted to the Republican party thereafter, until the New Deal. Following the unionization of the mines in the early thirties, Harlan became enthusiastically Democratic in national and state elections, but remained predominantly, though narrowly, Republican in local contests.

Wix Unthank, a Democrat, was county judge in 1955, the first Democrat to hold that office in Harlan for many years. Unthank was nominated despite the opposition of an Administration candidate and was elected without Administration support. Not unnaturally, therefore, he did not regard himself as an Administration man. However, he worked with the Administration when it was mutually advantageous and would certainly have enjoyed being named Administration man for the county.

Herb Smith was the county's long-time political leader and was the Administration man. Smith, unlike Nelson county's Sympson, was not a creature of the Administration, but was an independent political power in his own right. In the party primaries, the Administration could only hope that Smith would remember past favors and not "sell out" to the opposition.

Observers attributed Unthank's succession to the first office of the county to "whiskey, wedlock, and workers." By "wedlock" these observers had reference to the importance of the family in local politics. Traditionally there are some four or five well-to-do and/or prolific Harlan families which rule the county. Unthank belongs to one of these families and his wife to another. Therefore, in both the primary and general election the two families united in support of his candidacy.

The reasons for the importance attached to the position of county judge are various. One is the prestige of the position. For example, a struggling young lawyer's greatest need is for recognition in the community. A campaign for office is one means of advertising a name. A successful campaign for an important office provides stature in the community as well as recognition. But most importantly, the county judge has the power of the purse. To put it simply and crudely, the judge spends the county's money. Therefore, the friends of a successful candidate for the office of county judge do not jump up and down for joy on election night simply out of exuberance over their "team's" victory.

Herb Smith, the Harlan county "boss," was a man who had never held public office, but had become an almost legendary figure both in the state and Harlan county. Before the thirties, he was as uncompromisingly Republican as he was Democratic after 1932. Smith's first formal venture into the Democratic camp was in 1931 when he persuaded the mine operators that support of Ruby Laffoon, the Democratic candidate for governor, would be a wise business investment, in that the construction of roads to the mines would undoubtedly be a matter of first concern for the new Governor. The argument appealed to the operators' sense of the fitness of things and they followed his suggestion. A check of the official returns for 1931 reveals that the notation "Not properly Certified" is entered for Harlan county. Thus the Harlan vote was not counted at all, a satisfactory state of affairs from the point of view of the Laffoon people, for Harlan in those days generally registered awesome majorities for Republican candidates.

The Laffoon incident illustrates the foundations of Smith's power. Through the years he developed close relations with mine operators, union officials and state politicians. Because of these contacts, he was Administration man under the Laffoon, Chandler and Clements regimes. Prior to that he was associated with the Bi-Partisan Combine. As Administration man he enjoyed the same state road, state employment and state contracts authority previously described. However, because he was a full-time politician, with independent sources of support and funds, he was not tied to the administration as closely as was Bill Sympson of Nelson county. After "Happy" Chandler's election as governor in 1955, Smith remained an important political figure in the county.

3. Trigg County

Trigg county is a rural farm community located at the western end of the state. Trigg has been Democratic since before the Civil War and remained so oriented in 1955.

Smith Broadbent, Jr., was the Administration man in the county. Besides being Administration man, Broadbent was past president of the State Farm Bureau, a trustee of the University of Kentucky, and son of the largest landowner in the county. The Broadbent farm encompassed some 2,500 acres of the best land in the county. Broadbent, unlike some other political leaders, was not forced to rely upon political influence alone to swing the vote of Trigg county. In the tradition of the great landowner, he simply made a decision as to the identity of the better candidate, and then transmitted his decision to his suzerainty.

Broadbent's power stemmed from his economic position. He was father confessor to his people, paid their bills when they were in trouble, and performed favors for them when circumstances permitted. Frequently, the telephone at his home would ring in the early hours of the morning heralding a plea for assistance in some desperate emergency.

The duties performed by Broadbent as Administration man represented no more than an extension of his position as a great landowner and benevolent despot. It was he who selected applicants for work with the State Highway Department, decided where the roads were to be built and who was to get the state contracts. As Broadbent put it, "If it were your decision to make, wouldn't you build the road past your friend's house rather than your enemy's and hire your supporter rather than your detractor?"

Of course, Smith Broadbent, though the Administration man, was not the Administration's man. He was a free agent. If he felt that the Administration's candidate was a good one he would support him. If, for any reason, he decided to desert the Administration, it was not in a position to punish him.

In summary, the case studies of three representative Kentucky counties show that the political organization of the state is simple and direct. The governor enjoys the power of patronage and the purse. He, in turn, delegates this power to Administration men in the counties. In return, the Administration men are expected to support the governor and his candidates on election day, a support that does not always materialize.

There are two Kentucky election campaigns which illustrate rather well the extent of the Administration's authority at the local organizational level. One is the gubernatorial primary of 1935 when A. B. Chandler first stepped into the political spotlight, and the second is the 1949 effort to obtain the passage of a constitutional amendment revising upward the $5,000 limitation on the salaries of state officials.

In 1931, in the gubernatorial election immediately prior to the 1935 campaign, Ruby Laffoon, a Hopkins county Democrat, was the choice of the sovereign Kentucky electorate. Among the more enduring accomplishments of Laffoon's administration from 1931 to 1935 were the appointment of more Kentucky Colonels and the issuance of more pardons than in any previous Administration. But aside from making Mae West a Kentucky Colonel and emptying the prisons, Ruby Laffoon contributed to the folklore of the Commonwealth a series of breath-taking political blunders.

The first mistake made by Laffoon was to force upon his second legislature an unpopular and poorly conceived sales tax bill. By securing enactment of the sales tax immediately prior to the election campaign of 1935, he presented potential opponents of the Administration with a recent sore on the body politic susceptible to opportunistic exacerbation. The second and third mistakes made by Laffoon consisted in making it possible for just such an opportunist to successfully challenge his administration.

"Happy" Chandler, a rising young star of the time, was Laffoon's Lieutenant Governor. In 1934, "Happy" broke with the Laffoon administration and was forthwith "stripped" of his powers as Speaker of the Senate. Even at this early date, Chandler had at least one eye cocked toward the governor's mansion, but the prize seemed unattainable, for in any convention the Laffoon or Administration forces seemed certain to enjoy complete control (the party primary was optional before 1935). In 1935, however, Laffoon was guilty of a small indiscretion that was swiftly turned into a big one. Laffoon's mistake consisted in taking a trip to Washington to attend a meeting, thus leaving Chandler, the Lieutenant Governor, in control of the machinery of government.

The morning after Laffoon left the state, Chandler and a group of advisers closeted themselves in the governor's office. Following several hours of frantic activity, they emerged with a call for a special session of the legislature. The purpose of the call was the enactment of a compulsory primary law, replacing the existing permissive statute and thus enabling Chandler to run for the Democratic nomination as governor in a primary. All requirements of law were speedily satisfied and telegrams dispatched to the state's legislators summoning them to appear at a special meeting of the General Assembly. Laffoon hurriedly returned and attempted to render Chandler's call null and void. The Kentucky Court of Appeals, however, upheld the call's legality and further ruled that it was impossible for the governor to rescind it.

The culminating blunder of the Laffoon forces was committed during the legislative consideration of the primary law. According to the terms of the law proposed by the Chandler forces, only a simple majority was required for nomination. The Laffoon forces, however, decided that if the Chandler people wanted a primary law that they'd give them a "good" one. Thereupon, they proposed an amendment to the original bill requiring an absolute majority of all ballots cast for nomination and providing for a run-off between the two leading candidates in the event no candidate enjoyed such a majority.

This was a blunder of more than ordinary proportions because the advantage is almost always with the machine in a primary requiring but a simple majority. The Administration or machine candidate can always depend upon a sizeable block of votes even though he be the proverbial "yellow dog." These votes come from state employees, their relatives and their friends; and from people obligated to the Administration for one reason or another. If the machine can split the opposition by introducing a number of candidates in the primary, then victory is virtually assured for its candidate. Dan Talbott, who engineered passage of the bill for the Chandler forces, quickly accepted the Laffoon amendment.

The hills of Kentucky were then rocked by Chandler's mellifluous "Sonny Boy" as he vigorously campaigned for the nomination. In the first primary of 1935, the Administration's candidate, Tom Rhea of

Logan county, defeated Chandler, but fell several
thousand votes short of an absolute majority due to
the votes cast for several other candidates. Therefore,
a second primary was held from which Chandler
emerged victorious.[1]

In terms of political organization, the chief significance of the Democratic primary of 1935 lies in
the forces which opposed one another. On one side
was the Administration organization, generally referred
to as the Rhea-Laffoon machine, and on the other the
Chandler group which consisted of 1) a number of
organization people who had defected from the Laffoon
administration, such as Ben Johnson and Dan Talbott
of Nelson county, and Herb Smith of Harlan; and
2) an unusually large number of reform people who
were against the supposed excesses of the "machine."

Issues were of minimal importance in the primary.
Chandler concentrated his fire on the sales tax and
posed as the lonely antagonist of a powerful and
corrupt machine. Rhea largely confined himself to
"pointing with pride." The important thing about the
1935 primary, then, for the purposes of analysis is
that no great issues divided the electorate, such as
the "people" versus the corporations. Basically, the
campaign was between the Administration's organization and a candidate who represented himself as being
anti-machine.

Figure 4 identifies the counties carried by Rhea and
those by Chandler in the first primary contest. Figure
5 is an income map of the state which groups the

---

[1] In Kentucky, the governor cannot succeed himself, but invariably supports
a candidate for nomination and election. The person backed by the governor is
then called the Administration or organization candidate.

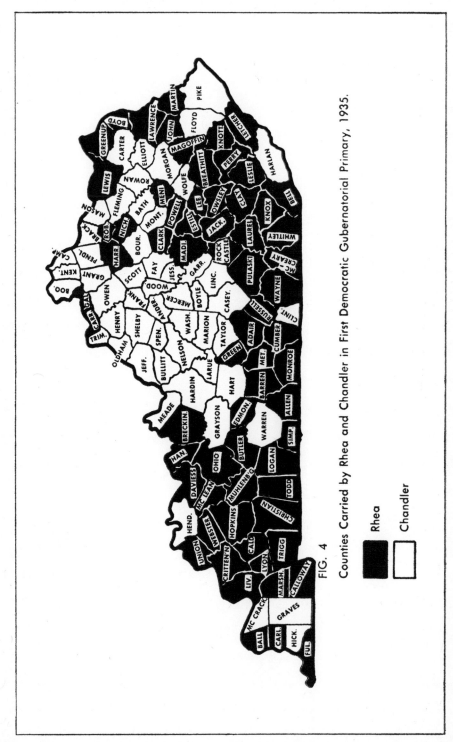

Counties Carried by Rhea and Chandler in First Democratic Gubernatorial Primary, 1935.

FIG. 4

■ Rhea

☐ Chandler

counties of the state according to income levels. The apparent relationship existing between Figures 4 and 5 is explored in Table 2.

Table 2 groups the counties of the state according to three categories: 1) whether they voted for Chandler or Rhea; 2) their political affiliation; 3) their income level. Reference to the table tells that Chandler did well in the more prosperous counties of the state and in the Democratic counties, whereas Rhea enjoyed overwhelming strength in both the poorer and Republican counties. Because the Republican counties in Kentucky are also its less prosperous communities, the question arises as to whether this isn't just two sides of the same coin.

Analysis convincingly demonstrates that both factors were operable in the primary. The differential response of Democratic and Republican counties to the two candidates is clear, as column 2 of Table 2 demonstrates. Chandler won 55 per cent of the state's Democratic counties, whereas he lost 80 per cent of the Republican counties. Turning to columns 3, 4, 5, and 6 of the table the relationship between the economic levels of the counties and their vote in the primary becomes equally incontrovertible. In both Democratic and Republican counties there was a positive correlation between economic level and the vote for Chandler. Among Democratic counties, only 37 per cent of the least wealthy counties cast a majority of their vote for Chandler, 40 per cent at the next highest level, 55 per cent at the next, and 75 per cent of the wealthiest Democratic counties registered their preference for Chandler's candidacy. Among Republican counties, Chandler won only 13 per cent of the poorest counties,

17 per cent at the next highest economic level, and 100 per cent of the more well-to-do Republican counties.

TABLE 2

RELATIONSHIP BETWEEN ECONOMIC LEVEL [1] AND POLITI-
CAL AFFILIATION OF COUNTIES [2] TO TENDENCY TO
CAST MAJORITY VOTE FOR CHANDLER AND RHEA
IN FIRST DEMOCRATIC GUBERNATORIAL
PRIMARY OF 1935

	Total No. Counties Carried	% Total Counties Carried	Economic Level							
			16-27% No. %		28-39% No. %		40-56% No. %		59%± No. %	
Dem. Counties:										
Chandler	47	55	3	37	6	40	23	55	15	75
Rhea	38	45	5	63	9	60	19	45	5	25
Totals	85	100	8	100	15	100	42	100	20	100
Rep. Counties:										
Chandler	7	20	2	13	3	17	1	100	1	100
Rhea	28	80	13	87	15	83	0	—	0	—
Totals	35	100	15	100	18	100	1	100	1	100
All Counties:										
Chandler	54	45	5	22	9	27	24	56	16	76
Rhea	66	55	18	78	24	73	19	44	5	24
Totals	120	100	23	100	33	100	43	100	21	100

[1] Economic level represents percentage of county's per capita income payments to United States average, 1939. Source: Will S. Meyers, Jr., John L. Johnson, and James W. Martin, *Kentucky Income Payments by Counties, 1939, 1947, 1950, and 1951*, Bureau of Business Research, Bulletin No. 26 (Lexington: University of Kentucky, 1953), p. 31.

[2] Counties are classified Democratic or Republican according to their most frequent affiliation in Presidential elections, 1932-52. Those counties which divided equally over the period were assigned to the party for which they cast the majority vote in 1952.

It is significant that even though the income factor was operable in both Democratic and Republican counties in the primary, Chandler fared substantially better in Democratic than in Republican counties at the low income levels. In addition, it should be noted that Chandler carried the only two Republican counties which were at a relatively high income level.

At first glance, the marked tendency of low income

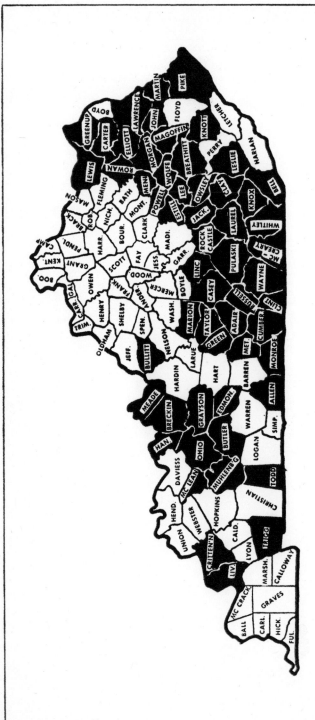

FIG. 5

Counties in Which Per Capita Income Payments to Individuals Were 39 Percent or Less of National Average, 1939. *

*Source: Will S. Myers, Jr., John L. Johnson, and James W. Martin, Kentucky Income Payments by Counties 1939, 1947, 1950, and 1951, Bureau of Business Research Bulletin No. 26 (Lexington: University of Kentucky, 1953), p. 31.

counties to cast their lot with the Rhea-Laffoon administration defies all logic. The only issue in the
campaign of any importance was the sales tax, which
Chandler opposed and Rhea defended. The sales tax
is almost universally regarded as a regressive tax with
nothing to recommend it from the point of view of
lower income groups. The mountain residents may
not have known that the tax was "regressive" but
nothing can be more certain than that they didn't
enjoy paying it. Almost any mountain person will
happily discourse at length on his aversion to the sales
tax, using as his frame of reference the Laffoon experiment.

The only variable offering an explanation for the
behavior of the low income counties is organization.
Whereas the Laffoon Administration was somewhat
inept in performing some of the rituals of government,
it was remarkably effective in matters of power and
organization. The use of state jobs and contracts as
political weapons was developed into a fine art by this
Administration. Stories are legion in Kentucky about
the appointments made, favors granted and money
expended in order to obtain the passage of Administration measures and to secure votes on election day.

In order to understand the role of organization in
the 1935 Democratic primary, it is helpful to refer to
the previous discussion of political organization at
the county level. It will be remembered that political
organization in Nelson, Harlan, and Trigg counties
was discussed. Two of these counties were carried by
Chandler in 1935, and the third, Trigg, cast a majority
of its vote for Tom Rhea, the Administration candidate. Because of the important roles played by the

political leaders of Nelson and Harlan counties in the primary it is instructive to reflect upon the reasons for the vote their counties cast.

Ben Johnson, the Nelson county political tyro, was a prominent figure in the Laffoon Administration in 1931. At the outset of the Administration he was given the key patronage and contract post of Commissioner of the Highway Department. However, Johnson's ambitions collided with Laffoon's determination to be his own governor. In short, Johnson was dismissed from his post as Highway Commissioner.

If his unceremonious departure from Laffoon's Administration had angered only Ben Johnson, Laffoon's political difficulties would have been great, but not insurmountable. But in back of Ben Johnson was a group of political leaders once known as the Bi-Partisan Combine. This formidable coalition of political leaders had made and unmade Kentucky governors for two decades, a phase of Kentucky political history which is discussed at length later in this chapter. The principal leaders of the Combine were located in the Bluegrass, urban centers, and coal counties, including Herb Smith of Harlan county. These people enjoyed intimate ties with the racetrack, coal, and liquor interests of the state, for whom they had fought many political battles.

The important point in this discussion is that Ben Johnson, Herb Smith, and the Bluegrass leaders were able to demand much of the Administration, and with little fear of possible retaliation by the governor. The governor was able to take from them some patronage, but they retained their tight grip upon the governments of their individual communities, and the related ties with leaders of the business community. Therefore, they were able to break with Laffoon with relative impunity and were in a position to groom and finance a challenger to the incumbent Administration. The individual they selected for this task was A. B. "Happy" Chandler.

Western Kentucky leaders, like Smith Broadbent, Sr., of Trigg county, supported the Administration candidate for two reasons. In the first place, Tom Rhea, the Administration candidate, was a resident of Logan county in western Kentucky and they supported him out of sectional loyalty. In the second and more important place, western Kentucky had long chafed under the yoke of Bluegrass, urban and coal domination of their party. Under Laffoon, who was from Hopkins county, western Kentucky received what it felt was long-overdue recognition in terms of patronage and contracts. They hoped to perpetuate this welcome change by electing Tom Rhea to succeed Laffoon.

The loyalty of the impoverished Eastern Mountain counties to the Administration is explicable by turning on its head the rationale for the defection of the Bluegrass counties. The political leaders of the less wealthy counties of the state are much more dependent upon the Administration for their political power than are leaders in wealthier communities. In a county where the per capita income payments to individuals are only 15 or 25 or 35 per cent of the national average, a position with the State Highway Department or a contract for the delivery of office equipment or a thousand dollars for use on election day assumes an importance of truly heroic proportions. The wise use of these emoluments of power in low income counties can result in the creation of a political machine of considerable potency. This is particularly true of Republican counties because in these the state employees are often the only Democratic party officials who take a day-to-day interest in politics. There are no local offices or patronage available to them independent of the patronage power of the governor. Therefore, in the party primaries the low-income counties are tied by close bonds of immediate self-interest to the Administration.

A test of the validity of the observations made is provided by the results of the second primary between Rhea and Chandler. If organization were a major factor in the vote of the low-income counties in the first primary, then in the second primary Rhea's vote should have been less affected in the low than in the high income counties by the trend toward Chandler, a trend that was evident throughout the state according to all observers.

A total of sixteen counties changed from Rhea to Chandler in the run-off primary. The low income counties, however, displayed remarkable resistance to the trend. Only 12 per cent of the low income counties (income level 39 per cent or less of national average) which were carried by Rhea in the first primary deserted his standard in the run-off, whereas 46 per cent of Rhea's wealthier counties switched to Chandler in the second primary. In terms of Democratic and Republican counties, only 7 per cent of the low income Republican counties changed to Chandler, but more than 20 per cent of Rhea's Democratic counties at the same economic level changed sides in the run-off primary. The results of the second primary thus tend to verify the contentions: 1) that low income counties are highly susceptible to political control emanating from without the county; and 2) that low income counties controlled by the Republican party are especially subject to such control in the Democratic primaries.

Another election which is of interest because of what it tells about the power structure in Kentucky politics is the 1949 vote on the constitutional amendment revising upward the $5,000 limitation on salaries.

TABLE 3

RELATIONSHIP OF 1950 INCOME LEVEL OF SELECTED KENTUCKY COUNTIES AND VOTE FOR 1949 CONSTITUTIONAL AMENDMENT [1]

	Mean % for Higher Salaries
10 Counties with Lowest Income Level [2]	60.3
10 Counties with Highest Income Level [3]	54.8
10 Counties with Modal Income Level [4]	45.9

[1] Income level represents percentage of county's per capita income payments to United States average, 1950. Source: Meyers, Johnson, Martin, *Kentucky Income Payments by Counties*, p. 31.

[2] Counties with per capita income payments 27% or less of national average, 1950.

[3] Counties with per capita income payments 75% or more of national average, 1950.

[4] Counties with per capita income payments 43 through 47% of national average, 1950.

Table 3 tells a story as ironic as any passage written by Balzac. If the "Official Statement of the Tabulated Vote" issued by Kentucky's Secretary of State is to be believed, the voters of the very poorest counties of the state greeted the idea of raising the salaries of state officials with more undisguised enthusiasm than did the residents of the cities. As shown by Table 3, it was the poor and the rich counties which tended to support the amendment, whereas the middle income counties tended to vote against it.

Further light is thrown on the nature of political organization in the Eastern Mountains by the vote on the 1949 constitutional amendment. In these low income mountain counties, as in certain big city wards of a comparable economic level, there is a habit of long duration of taking certain liberties with the vote of the not-so-sovereign electorate. A state official tells with some amusement of a phone call he received from an excited election official the night the vote was tabulated for and against the 1949 constitutional amendment. The election official was in one of the mountain counties and he was upset. It seemed that his fellow election officials felt that good sense, not to mention good taste, demanded that they limit the majority reported for the amendment to 2,000 votes. The election official, however, anxious to make a good impression, was holding out for a majority of 4,000 votes. The purpose of the call was to ask the state official to intervene with a demand that the higher figure prevail.

The focus of this study turns next to social and economic divisions of the Kentucky electorate. It will be helpful to keep in mind what has been learned of political organization in the low income counties as the nature of the state's social and economic divisions unfolds. Otherwise, the vote of the low income counties in elections dividing the electorate along social and economic lines is inexplicable.

Social and Economic Divisions

In the preceding pages political organization in Kentucky has been examined, as it were, in a vacuum. In the succeeding pages the Kentucky political scene shall be analyzed *in toto*. This will be accomplished by adding to the cast of characters thus far introduced, the interest groups and some of their leaders; people who have played an important part in Kentucky politics.

The basic division within the Democratic party in Kentucky is between the rural folk and the eastern Kentucky urban and Bourbon people. It was in the elections during the last decade of the nineteenth century that the farmers of western Kentucky first challenged Bourbon control of the Democratic party in the state.

Before the Civil War the slaveholders, centered in the Bluegrass (see Figure 6 for a map of Kentucky's economic areas), ruled the state. The coalition by means of which this group secured and maintained power consisted of the Bourbons in the Bluegrass and the Pennyroyal, in combination with the poor folk of the Eastern and Western Mountains and the South-central Knobs.

Following the Civil War the same ex-slaveholders or Bourbons remained in power, but by means of a new coalition. Reconstruction forced the ex-slaveholding Whigs into the Democratic party, but their mountain friends remained true to the principles of Clay and moved from the Whig party into the party of Lincoln. The Inner Bluegrass Bourbons found it necessary, therefore, to align themselves with the farmers of western Kentucky and the Outer Bluegrass, people who had called themselves Democratic since the election of 1828. The new coalition ruled uninterruptedly until the advent of Populism in the closing decade of the century.

Henry Watterson's "New South" brought a new type of Bourbon to the Bluegrass. The new Bourbon was the corporation owner, and he demanded and obtained a share in the councils of the old slavocracy. The old Bourbons and the new found little difficulty in making common cause. They had an equal interest in sound money and conservative government, and, besides, the old Bourbons were often investors in the corporate plantations of the new.

The small farmer of western Kentucky, however, found the new Bourbons indigestible. High freight rates and depression were the precipitants which brought the conflict of interests to a decision. The Farmers' Alliance was formed in Kentucky in 1889 and a Populist candidate was entered in the gubernatorial elections of 1891 and 1895. Defection of western Kentucky Democrats to the Populist candidate in protest against the presence of a gold Democrat on the ticket was sufficient in 1895 to elect a Republican governor for the first time since the Civil War.

In 1896 the western farmers were happy with William Jennings Bryan, the Democratic party's presidential nominee, but the Bluegrass defected to the Republican nominee in company with the mountain people of eastern Kentucky. The pattern of the elections of 1895 and 1896 is one that recurs. And it is very nearly the same picture that existed prior to the Civil War; i.e., the Bluegrass and Eastern Mountains allied against the remainder of the state.

The gubernatorial election of 1899 provided the cli-

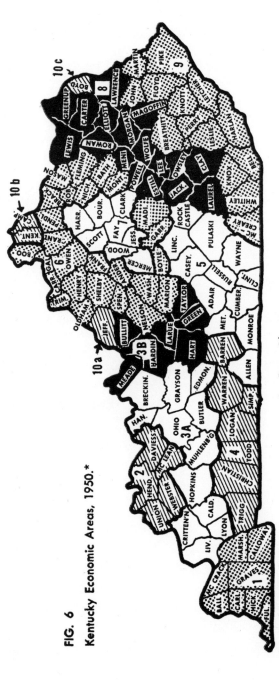

FIG. 6

Kentucky Economic Areas, 1950.*

1. Jackson Purchase
2. Owensboro-Henderson
3a. Western Coal and Mountains
3b. Eastern Pennyroyal and Knobs
4. Pennyroyal
5. Southcentral Knobs

6. Outer Bluegrass
7. Inner Bluegrass
8. Eastern Mountains
9. Eastern Coal and Mountains
10a, b, c. Metropolitan counties of a) Jefferson, b) Kenton and Campbell, and c) Boyd.

*Source: Paul D. Richardson and James S. Brown, Population Estimates for Kentucky Counties, April 1, 1953, Kentucky Agricultural Experiment Station, Progress Report 14 (Lexington: University of Kentucky, 1953), p. 10.

mactic struggle between the forces of western and eastern Kentucky, or between the middle-income farmers
and the Bourbons. This contest was, by all accounts,
the most acrimonious in the history of the state. The
heat generated by the election and subsequent events
left a residue of bitterness that endured for many years.

William Goebel was the nominee of the Democratic
party.   Goebel's principal antagonist in both the
Democratic convention and the election was the Louisville and Nashville Railroad. A machine politician
from Covington, Goebel knew all the tricks of the
game and made use of them. He obtained the gubernatorial nomination at a riotous convention in Louisville's Music Hall, by the simple device of securing
control of the machinery of the affair and thereupon
ejecting the delegates of his principal opponent (backed
by the L&N).

Milton H. Smith, President of the Louisville and
Nashville Railroad in 1899, and Goebel's principal
antagonist, provides a vivid description of Goebel the
man and the politician. "He was a most remarkable
man," according to Smith,

> from the fact that he dominated by will or by
> force, the people. He didn't try to conciliate any-
> body; he would almost insult a man who would
> curry favor with him. I recall one instance—he
> was eating dinner at the Inn, a rather popular
> restaurant here, and a man who had an industry
> or business house where there were ten or twelve
> votes that he thought he could control, sought to
> tell him of it, and Goebel insulted him and the
> man went away angry. He was a strange com-
> bination, and I will say that it was my expecta-
> tion that he would be killed, and I think that it
> was so with others, because he was reckless in his

manner of treating people . . . I will relate one instance as showing the recklessness of the man: there was a Democrat (and he is still a Democrat and a very prominent one in this state—and an officeholder, too, and his father had been before him) who had some reputation of being a man-handler, because I think when a young man he had killed someone—I don't know much about it. He was looking after certain matters at Frankfort, and returning to his hotel after midnight was told that Mr. Goebel wanted to see him. He went to Mr. Goebel's room with his overcoat on. He was a very spare man. There was another man there from the western part of the state. Goebel locked the door and said, "Are you armed?" The fellow threw open his overcoat and said; "As well as any man in Kentucky," displaying two revolvers and a bowie knife. Presenting his revolvers, he said: "Open the door!" Goebel opened the door and he withdrew. He was very angry, . . . Undoubtedly, Goebel, in endeavoring to intimidate ran a great risk and it is a wonder that he was not killed. General Duke [an attorney and political adviser for the L&N] who was up there . . . [in Frankfort concerning Goebel's contesting of the election returns] carried a derringer in his pocket. He expected that Goebel would assault him. He would be eating at the breakfast table, and Goebel would come around glaring at him. Knowing that these things were going on, it was naturally expected that he would either kill somebody or be killed, but nobody, so far as I know, anticipated his assassination![1]

Goebel's platform in 1899 included planks pledging railroad regulation and, specifically, strict control of

---

[1] From Transcript of Interview of Milton H. Smith, President of the Louisville and Nashville Railroad Company, by C. P. Connolly, representing Hearst Magazines, Oct. 6, 1913 (unpublished), sent to Dr. Bennett H. Wall, Professor, University of Kentucky, by Sidney Smith, Vice-president of the L&N, pp. 52-53.

the L&N; cheap freight rates for farmers; free text-
books; and continuing advocacy of free silver. At one
point, Goebel told his audience:

> I have no doubt that if in the Louisville con-
> vention I had permitted Mr. Milton H. Smith and
> Mr. August Belmont [L&N officials] to run the
> L&N political locomotive over me, in their judg-
> ment I would be an entirely proper person, not
> only to be governor of Kentucky, but to hold any
> other place within the gift of the people. But I
> did not see fit to do that. It has not been my
> custom to permit anything to run over me, and
> you can depend on it that I shall not permit the
> L&N locomotive to run over me on the 7th of
> next November.[1]

Goebel's objective seemed to be the formation of a
farmer-labor coalition, for he was relying upon the
Populist vote of western Kentucky combined with the
urban vote of his home Kenton-Campbell county area
across the river from Cincinnati, for victory. However,
on November 8, 1899, the L&N political locomotive
thought that it had, indeed, "run over" Mr. Goebel.
The official count, and it remains so to this day, was
193,000 for Taylor, the Republican hopeful, to 191,000
for Goebel.

Taylor was subsequently inaugurated as governor of
the Commonwealth, but Goebel obstinately refused to
believe that the official ballot count was quite accurate.
Indeed, he was so married to this opinion that the
legislature, immediately upon convening, appointed a
Commission to investigate alleged irregularities. In
alarm, the *L&N* thereupon issued broadside to Republican partisans in the mountains invitations to a free

---

[1] Thomas D. Clark, "The People, William Goebel, and the Kentucky Railroads," *The Journal of Southern History*, Vol. V, No. 1 (February 1939), p. 44.

ride to Frankfort. These mountain folk descended on the State capital " . . . armed with standard equipment for a Kentucky gentleman of that time, a '44' Colt revolver, a Winchester rifle, a jug of corn liquor, and a pack of cards." [1]

In rapid succession, thereafter, Goebel was shot, sworn in as governor, reigned for four days, and died on February 3, 1900. The Democratic Lieutenant Governor, J. C. W. Beckham, was then sworn in as governor. The deposed Republican Governor, William S. Taylor, decided at about this time that discretion was the better part of remaining in Kentucky, and left for Indiana. Taylor spent his declining years in the haven of Republican Indiana, safe from Democratic warrants for his arrest.

During the eight years that Beckham shouldered the burdens of the office of governor he did nothing to injure the rather sensitive feelings of those who had so bitterly opposed his running mate. In fact, as Figure 7 indicates, he enjoyed the support of the L&N Railroad in the gubernatorial election of 1903. Figure 7 tells the story of Beckham's successful candidacy in 1903. According to the map, Beckham in 1903 enjoyed the most pronounced recrudescence in Democratic strength over Goebel's showing in 1899 in the counties along the route of the railroads where the L&N's political strength was greatest.

Milton Smith, once again, provides an authoritative account of the process by which a truce was arranged between the L&N, Governor Beckham, and the Democratic party:

---

[1] *Ibid.*, p. 45.

FIG. 7

Comparison of Routes of Selected Railroad Lines and Percentage-Point Increase in Democratic Vote by Counties in Gubernatorial Elections, 1899-1903.

::::: Selected Railroad Lines*

■ Percentage-Point Increase of 4 or more in Democratic Percentage of Total Vote.

*Source: Kincaid, A. Herr, The Louisville and Nashville Railroad, 1850-1942, L & N Magazine, Louisville, Kentucky, 1943, p. 42.

[After Goebel's assassination] things quieted down, and along in May following a man who had been prominent in the state, especially on Goebel's side, came to see me and deprecated the fact that the L&N Railroad Company was fighting the Democratic party. I said: "Suppose you turn that around. Why should the Democratic party fight the L&N Railroad Company? Why not let us go along and tend to our business? Damn the Democrats. Damn the Republicans. It is nothing but a dirty scramble to see who shall hold the offices. We are not wanting offices—we are not office holders, and we are not office seekers." "Now," I said, "Suppose you stop this. Things are in such a condition that people are afraid to come into the state. The L&N Railroad Company is taxing its credit to the utmost to obtain money with which to make extensions and additions, but not one dollar is being expended by it in the state of Kentucky. Now let the Democratic party with their interests join with the L&N Railroad Company in trying to do something to promote the material interests of the state." He replied that he would like to do that. "Then," I said, "get busy. Who shall we see about it?" He said, "A party at Owensboro." I said, "He is all right." He suggested Senator Blackburn, and I said I would see him. I said, "Here is a newspaper down at Glasgow." He said, "Well, we will stop that." I said, "Now you have people going about the state abusing the corporations, and you are going to have a convention at Lexington. Shut them off—don't let them abuse the corporations." The procedure suggested was followed. . . . [1]

Thus the Bourbons were the victors in their first clash with a coalition of western Kentucky farmers

---

[1] From Transcript of Interview between Milton Smith, President of L&N, and C. P. Connolly, Oct. 6, 1913, Unpublished, pp. 53-54.

and the labor and immigrant vote of northern Kentucky. They won by the pre-Civil War tactic of allying with the poor folk of the Eastern and Western Mountains and by carrying the Bluegrass by a large margin. The fight was unequal, for the Bourbons were able to use the Republican party as a weapon in the intraparty row. The Bourbons, after losing the intraparty fight with Goebel and Bryan, carried the day by threatening the Democratic party with defeat by the Republican party. However, in good times or bad it is extremely difficult for a western Kentucky leader to carry a traditionally Democratic county for the Republican party, except through a device such as the interjection of a third party.

Between 1900 and 1923, the Bourbons ruled Kentucky's Democratic party and the state. During this period there was born a coalition of political leaders who were identified with the Bourbons, and which was known as the Bi-Partisan Combine. It was in the gubernatorial elections of 1907 and 1919 when Republican gubernatorial candidates were elected that the existence of such a combine first became apparent. The chief source of Democratic sorrow and Republican elation in these elections was the insane oscillations in the percentage Democratic vote in the urban counties of Jefferson (containing the city of Louisville), Kenton, and Campbell. In the elections of 1907 and 1919, in these three counties, the percentage Democratic vote declined in the neighborhood of 10 percentage points over the preceding gubernatorial elections, an almost unheard of percentage-point gyration.

Obviously, the Democratic and Republican leaders of the urban communities, acting in concert, had learned that by effective use of the concentrated and malleable urban voting populace they could effect a victory for either side in a close election, and all elections were close during this period of Kentucky's political history.[1] This power served as a fulcrum whereby the leaders of the urban communities imposed their wishes on both parties. It was an exhibition of power politics that did not escape the attention of other politicians in the state.

The Bi-Partisan Combine that was formed in the 1920's was developed from this original grouping of political leaders in the urban centers, and, in addition, included political leaders from the population centers of the Bluegrass and the Eastern Coal section.

Bi-partisan has become a "good word" in the vocabulary of American politics. The reader, however, should forthwith disabuse his mind of any such prejudice with reference to the Bi-Partisan Combine. Kentucky's Bi-Partisan Combine was definitely not a league devoted to the promotion of the cause of good government.

The Combine possessed four important and distinctive attributes: 1) It was non-partisan. Non-partisan in this instance means that party victory was unimportant to the members of the group on election day. Billy Klair of Lexington was a Democrat, and

---

[1] The rigidity and the narrowness of the division between the two parties in the rural areas of the state during this period were extraordinary. In Presidential elections from 1896 through 1924 the percentage Democratic vote of the two-party vote in the state outside the four metropolitan counties and the Eastern coal counties was as follows:

1896	1900	1904	1908	1912*	1916	1920	1924
54%	53%	54%	53%	52%	54%	54%	53%

* Progressive party vote is included in Republican vote, 1912.

Morris Galvin of Covington was of the opposite political faith. But to these two gentlemen, and to other members of the Combine, the nomination and election of Combine candidates was infinitely more important than party success. If both candidates were Combine nominees then a friendly contest would ensue for the benefit and edification of the faithful. However, if one party should by some grievous oversight fail to nominate the candidate of their choice, then it was no contest so far as they were concerned. 2) The leaders of the Combine were political bosses from population centers of the state, and thus in a position to manipulate a considerable body of votes. 3) The state was very evenly divided between the Democratic and Republican parties. 4) The Combine was closely identified with and supported by the racetrack, coal and liquor interests of the state.

In 1923, a Don Quixote came charging out of the grassy fields of western Kentucky to do battle with the racetrack, liquor and coal buzzsaw. Alben Barkley from Paducah, Kentucky, at the western tip of the state, was the "white knight" of the campaign. Barkley opposed Cantrill, the Combine candidate, in the Democratic gubernatorial primary of 1923.[1] Barkley's campaign planks in the primary included pledges to levy a production tax on coal and outlaw pari-mutuel betting. In addition to committing himself to these cardinal sins, Barkley was hotly "dry" and emphatically anti-machine.

The Combine candidate defeated Barkley in the primary by a margin of about 9,000 votes out of a

---

[1] Before 1935, the candidates could be selected by either a party convention or a primary.

total cast of some 240,000. Barkley carried virtually the entire state west of Carroll county on the north and Bell county on the south (a line which virtually divides the state in half), whereas Cantrill, the Combine candidate, swept every county but two east of these points (see Figure 8). Cantrill enjoyed overwhelming margins in the Inner Bluegrass, the Eastern Coal section and in the urban area of Jefferson (Louisville), Kenton (Covington), and Campbell (Newport) counties. The margin for Cantrill in Kenton, though less than in the other urban communities named, was a comfortable 63 per cent. It is significant that eleven of the fourteen Eastern Mountain and Coal counties carried by Cantrill by two-thirds or more were Republican. The only Democratic counties in the section to give Cantrill a one-sided victory were Breathitt, Wolfe and Powell counties, whereas Morgan, Elliott, Menifee, Floyd and Knott, all Democratic counties, cast less lopsided margins in support of the Combine candidate.

Barkley's defeat did not end the revolt of the state's small farmers against bi-partisan Bluegrass, coal and urban domination of the Democratic party. In 1927, J. C. W. Beckham, the lieutenant governor at Goebel's death, reappeared on the Kentucky political scene in the role of another reform candidate. Despite the apparent inconsistencies in his political career, Beckham bravely remounted the literally bloody horse of reform from which Goebel had been shot and Barkley rudely removed.

The issues in the Democratic primary of 1927 were virtually the same as those of 1923. Beckham advocated a production tax on coal and the abolition of pari-mutuel betting as had Barkley, while his Combine-supported opponent, Crowe, accused him of insincerity and worse. This time, however, the Combine faced a candidate who enjoyed rank and file support throughout the state because of his identification with the Goebel episode and long years of public service as governor and United States Senator. Beckham emerged victorious in the primary by a vote of 167,000 to 138,000 for his Combine-supported opponent.

In 1927, as in 1923, the Combine-supported candidate's strength was concentrated in eastern Kentucky, whereas the "reform" candidate's support was greatest in the western part of the state. In Table 4 the relation between the vote for Barkley in 1923 and that for Beckham in 1927 is explored. As Table 4 shows, both Barkley and Beckham carried more than 80 per cent of the western Kentucky counties, whereas both candidates lost more than 60 per cent of the Urban and Inner Bluegrass, and Eastern Mountain counties. The Outer Bluegrass was ambivalent in its vote and experienced a more pronounced swing to the anti-Combine candidate in 1927 than did any other section of the state. Barkley carried 31 per cent of the Outer Bluegrass counties, whereas Beckham won 73 per cent of these counties. It is interesting to note that the Republican counties were divided in almost identical proportions in the 1923 and 1927 primaries, whereas there was a pronounced swing to Beckham in the Democratic counties in the 1927 primary. Barkley carried only 48 per cent of the state's Democratic counties, whereas Beckham carried 76 per cent of the same counties. Beckham's support in Republican

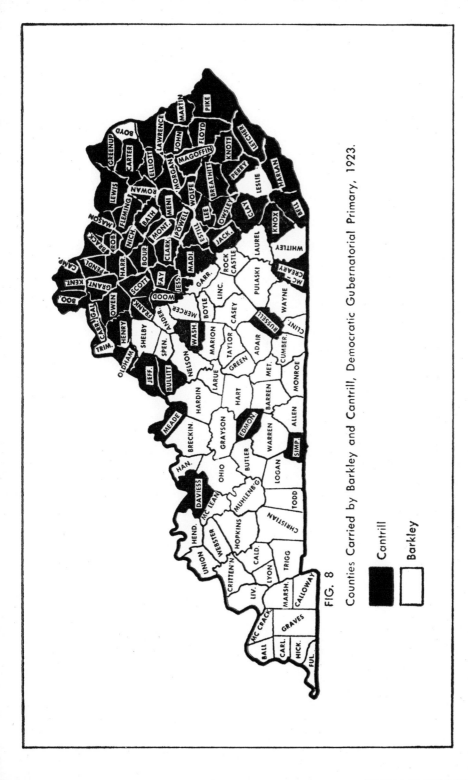

FIG. 8

Counties Carried by Barkley and Cantrill, Democratic Gubernatorial Primary, 1923.

Cantrill

Barkley

counties was only six percentage points greater than that given Barkley.

It might be a logical premise that Barkley's strength in the western part of the state was a sectional vote, rather than a division on economic issues, because Barkley's home was in the Jackson Purchase section at the extreme western tip of the state. However, the

TABLE 4
KENTUCKY — A THREE PARTY STATE
Kentucky Counties by Sections and Vote for Barkley and Beckham in the Gubernatorial Primaries of 1923 and 1927

		The State	Western Kentucky	Outer Bluegrass	Urban and Inner Bluegrass	Eastern Coal and Mountains
Total No. of Counties		120	50	26	11	33
Counties Carried	No.	51	42	7	1	1
by Both	% of Counties of Section	42	82	27	9	3
Counties Lost	No.	35	1	6	7	21
by Both	%	29	2	23	64	66
Carried by Beckham and Lost by Barkley	No.	28	6	12	3	7
	%	23	12	46	27	22
Carried by Barkley and Lost by Beckham	No.	6	2	1	0	3
	%	5	4	4	0	9
Total Carried	No.	57	44	8	1	4
by Barkley	%	47	86	31	9	12
Total Carried	No.	79	48	19	4	8
by Beckham	%	66	94	73	36	25

Democratic Counties: [1]
  Carried by
    Barkley % 48
    Beckham % 76
Republican Counties: [1]
  Carried by
    Barkley % 47
    Beckham % 53

[1] Counties are classified Democratic or Republican according to their most frequent affiliation in the Presidential elections, 1896-1928.

correspondence between the vote for Beckham and
Barkley destroys this premise, because Beckham was
a blueblooded Bluegrasser. Therefore, the results of
the two campaigns provide persuasive evidence that
the vote was at least partially based on the issues of
the campaigns.

It is important, however, to note that seventy-five
per cent of the counties that were carried by Beckham and lost by Barkley are located in the Inner and
Outer Bluegrass and Eastern Mountain sections of
the Commonwealth. If it had not been for this eastern
Kentucky strength Beckham would probably have
been defeated. Significantly, the eastern Kentucky
counties in which Beckham fared well relative to
Barkley's showing were primarily Democratic counties.
In the Eastern Mountain section, nine of the ten
counties that voted against both Barkley and Beckham
were Republican by complexion, whereas four of the
six counties that cast majorities for Beckham and not
Barkley were Democratic.

The support Beckham received in the Bluegrass and
Eastern Mountains was probably a result of the following factors: 1) Beckham was a native of the Bluegrass. His home was in Nelson county where he lived
at the manorial "Home of Three Governors," in the
tradition and spirit of the blueblooded country squire.
It is not surprising then that he was the recipient of
considerable Bluegrass support in spite of his rather
eccentric points of view. It must be remembered that
Barkley was a little-known Congressman from the
western tip of the state whose opponent was a native
of the Bluegrass; whereas Beckham was a blueblooded
Bluegrasser grown old in the state's service who faced

a rather obscure figure from Oldham county. 2) During his eight years as governor and six as United States Senator Beckham enjoyed many opportunities to perform favors for Democratic friends and party workers. Thus 3) many Democratic leaders in the Democratic counties of eastern Kentucky were motivated to disregard the wishes of the machine and support Beckham. In both primaries Democratic leaders in Democratic counties were more prone to defy the machine than their counterparts in Republican counties, as is shown by the fact that 60 per cent of the counties lost by both Barkley and Beckham were Republican, whereas 60 per cent of those captured by both hopefuls were of the Democratic faith.

Despite the defeat suffered by it in the primary, the Combine entered the general election unterrified. The Republican candidate for governor was Flem (sometimes known as "Flim Flam") Sampson, who hailed from the Eastern Coal county of Knox. Sampson was the Combine's candidate in the general election. Stories about the campaign that followed are legion in Kentucky. People who were participants claim that the Jockey Club invested one million dollars or more in the election of Sampson. The Jockey Club was, and is, composed of prominent Bluegrassers interested in promoting the "sport of kings." These "kings" look with a dim view on any proposals involving the taxation or elimination of pari-mutuel betting.

A high state official tells of a Bi-Partisan Combine meeting with which he is personally acquainted at which the Jockey Club presented the Combine leaders with $500,000. According to this official, the money was spent with considerable sagacity by the Combine.

Instead of spending the Jockey Club money on demagogic appeals to the prejudices of the voters they went, as a rational economic man might, straight to the source of election figures, i.e., the election officials, in an effort to create a climate of opinion favorable to the superior claims of Mr. Sampson to the office of governor.

The scene on that November day in 1927 was probably similar to occurrences on the election day in 1949 when the Administration made its heroic and successful effort to amend the constitutional $5,000 limitation on salaries. The election officials "counted" the ballots busily, and Beckham was defeated by a comfortable margin, and the state left safe for bourbon, horses and coal. Sampson's victory margin was some 30,000 votes. Beckham was defeated in the general election by roughly the same constellation of forces that opposed him in the primary, that defeated Barkley in the 1923 primary, and that defeated Bryan in the state in 1896. The Inner Bluegrass, northern urban counties, Eastern Coal and Mountain counties all returned Democratic votes sharply reduced over those given the Combine-approved Democratic candidate of 1923. Even Nelson county, Beckham's home county, defected from its favorite son in terms of the size of its Democratic majority. The reason for the slap at Beckham in his home county was that Ben Johnson, a Combine member from Nelson county whose political exploits have been commented upon, worked for Beckham's defeat with more than ordinary enthusiasm, due to a personal dislike it is said he harbored for his blueblooded neighbor.

The gubernatorial election of 1927 marked the close

of a chapter in the state's political history. Since 1927, no candidate has presented himself who has seriously challenged the position of the ruling oligarchy of the state. It is safe to predict, however, that if similar issues were to arise again the division of the state would be roughly comparable to that of the twenties, with the possible exception of the Eastern Coal counties which, with unionization, possess a new power structure with somewhat different objectives and orientations from those owned by the operators who formerly controlled the counties.

Conclusions

In analyzing Kentucky's political organization, the thesis developed was that the Democratic counties of the state tend to be more independent in Democratic primaries than are the state's Republican counties. Similarly, there seems to be a relationship between the wealth of a community and its political independence in primaries. The evidence indicates that the causes of these political phenomena are: 1) the political leaders in the Democratic counties have access to local patronage, whereas the Democratic leaders in Republican counties must depend upon the state administration for the sugar and spice that political organization is made of; 2) in wealthy counties the political leaders enjoy access to local sources of campaign contributions, whereas political leaders in impoverished communities must look elsewhere for the wherewithal to fight political battles.

The importance of these facts of political organization becomes apparent upon moving to the larger stage of the basic social and economic cleavages in the state.

In the Populist controversy of the late nineteenth century, and in the gubernatorial campaigns of the 1920's, the political war between Kentucky's divergent economic groups took place on two levels. On one level an effort was made to rally the people of the state behind opposing viewpoints. At this level it was an ideological conflict. On one side were those who, like Henry Watterson and the President of the Louisville and Nashville Railroad, were advocates of the "New South." They regarded themselves as the state's genuine progressives, engaged as they were in "rescuing" the state from the "dead hand" of rural rule. On the other side were men like Goebel and Barkley, who articulated the resentment of the urban workers and the yeoman farmers of the state against the "excesses" of the corporations, and who preached the necessity of regulation.

The second level at which these campaigns were fought was that of organization. In 1899, Kenton and Campbell counties supported Goebel, the champion of taxation and regulation of the corporations. After Goebel's death these counties entered the lists in support of the principles which Goebel opposed. It would be academic to debate which point of view most accurately represented the sentiments of the community. The important point is that when Goebel controlled the organization they voted one way, and after Goebel's death reversed their position. Similarly, in every clash of interest groups discussed, the Eastern Mountain counties were found on the side of the Bourbons. This political behavior is incomprehensible unless seen in the perspective of political organization. The Bourbons control the Eastern Mountain counties because they stand at the source of the patronage, contracts, and money on which the local organizations depend for their survival. Similarly, the political leaders of urban communities find that the corporations are more generous than other groups in the amounts of their contributions and thus tend to represent the points of view of their benefactors.

Unlike states of the Deep South (until recently), the defeated side in Democratic intraparty rows in Kentucky have a second line of defense. By deserting the Democratic standard in the general election they can make the victory of their opponents in the primaries a Pyrrhic one. Therefore, Kentucky and the other Border States are characterized as three-party states in these pages. The important contests to determine "Who shall rule" take place within the ranks of the Democratic party. However, the Republican party stands ever ready to seize the reins of government if Democratic hands become too vigorously engaged in pummeling fellow Democrats.

CHAPTER III
KENTUCKY TRENDS

K ENTUCKY is a Border State. As such, the political environment is unique, partaking as it does of elements of the cultures of both North and South. In Chapter II, the struggle for power within the distinctive Border State environment was viewed from the perspective of political organization and the economic divisions of the populace. Necessarily, attention was centered upon manipulation and groupings of economic and political leaders in explaining shifts in the relative strength of the major parties in elections. However, the political change induced by manipulation and political organization is not, in and of itself, likely to endure. "Counting" may win an election or a group of elections, but it seldom affects the fundamental predispositions of the electorate.

In this chapter attention will be centered upon the type of political change that endures and becomes a part of the environment within which the political game, as described in Chapter II, is played. An effort will be made to determine the location of long-term political change in Kentucky, and to isolate some of the variables responsible.

The Background

Kentucky's political structure has its foundation in four events; the "Age of Jackson," the Civil War, the Populist period, and the Great Depression. The division of Kentucky's electorate between the Democratic and Republican parties is, in large part, a result of the reactions of various elements of the state's population to these four events.

According to Figure 9, the political loyalties of 75 of Kentucky's 120 counties were fixed at or before the Civil War (11 additional counties have voted consistently Republican since 1896). The traditionally Democratic counties identified in Figure 9 are concentrated in three areas of the state: 1) western Kentucky in the Jackson Purchase (the extreme western tip of the state) and the Henderson county area; 2) the Outer Bluegrass; and 3) the northcentral Eastern Mountains. Traditional Republican strength, on the other hand, is located in the Eastern Mountains and the Southcentral Knobs regions. The long-term Republican and Democratic counties tend to be predominantly rural. In the one-sidedly Democratic and Republican counties an average of 55 per cent of the population consists of rural farm people, compared with a figure of 33 per cent for the state.

The majority (48) of the 75 counties which have been loyally Democratic or Republican since the Civil War were, respectively, Democratic and Whig strongholds during the Jackson period.[1] The people of the Northern (Outer) Bluegrass and Jackson Purchase sections joined with Andrew Jackson in his opposition to Bourbon rule because they wanted to be left alone to till their fertile farms. They remain predominantly Democratic. Their mountain brethren, however, allied themselves with the Bourbon Whigs out of a desire to obtain internal improvements. An additional explanation for the pre-Civil War Whig alignment of

---

[1] Counties not formed before the Civil War are assigned to the political affiliation of their mother counties.

many mountain counties is their notorious susceptibility to the type of political argument that the well-
to-do are in a position to advance. Surprisingly, or
perhaps not so surprisingly, the Republican counties
as a group are economically depressed, whereas the
Democratic are relatively prosperous. In 1950, the 30
traditionally Republican counties had a mean per capita
income which was 32 per cent of the national average,
compared with a relative economic level of 50 per cent
for the 56 long-time Democratic counties.

Therefore, the Civil War, though a base point in the
politics of the state, cannot be regarded as the ex-
clusive determinant of the political coloration of the
counties. The Civil War accentuated the Democratic
loyalties of the people of the Northern Bluegrass and
Jackson Purchase sections because they had their roots
in the South and tended to support slavery as an institution; and made more pronounced the Whig or
Republican proclivities of the mountain people because
of their strong loyalty to the Union and lack of interest
in or sympathy with slavery. But the War did not
entirely reshape the political spectrum of the state.

The most important effect wrought by the Civil War
on the political complexion of Kentucky was the political change that occurred in the once-great slave
centers. This change finds but little reflection in the
political divisions recorded in Figure 9 because of its
compensatory nature. In sum, the Civil War tended
to make Democrats of the Bourbons and Republicans
of the former slaves, thus making the Bourbon counties politically marginal, though inclined Democratic.
Kentucky's slave centers were located in the Inner
Bluegrass (Fayette and surrounding counties), and

FIG. 9

The One-Sidedly Democratic and Republican Counties,
Based upon Presidential Elections, 1872-1952.

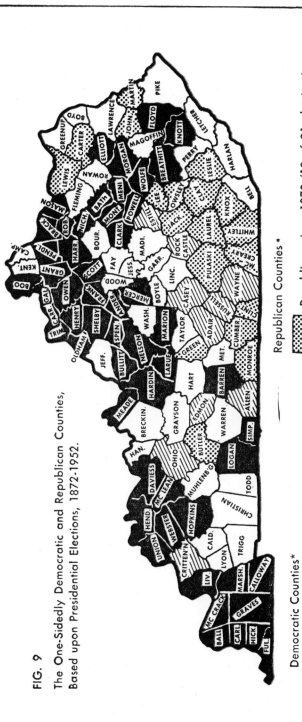

Democratic Counties*

■ Democratic since 1872 (19 of 21 elections).

Republican Counties*

▦ Republican since 1872 (19 of 21 elections).

▨ Republican since 1896 (14 of 15 elections).

*Progressive and Republican vote in 1912 are
grouped as Republican.

*Counties are assigned vote of mother county prior
to formation.

the Pennyroyal (Christian and surrounding counties). The effect of the colored vote on the relative strength of the two major political parties is made evident by a comparison of the percentage Democratic vote in the presidential elections of 1868 and 1872.

In Table 5, fifty-four counties with a significant percentage of Negroes in their 1870 voting population

TABLE 5 [1]

THE KENTUCKY NEGRO VOTED REPUBLICAN
Comparison of Presidential Elections of 1868 and 1872 in Kentucky Counties with Negro Population 3 per cent of Total or More

No. of Counties	Percentage-point Decrease in Democratic Vote, 1868-1872	Mean Negro Percentage of Potential Vote
12	10-19	7.6
16	20-29	15.7
17	30-39	26.3
8	40-49	29.1
1	50-59	33.9

[1] Adapted from Table in J. B. Shannon, *Presidential Politics in Kentucky* (Lexington: University of Kentucky, 1950), pp. 45-46.

(three per cent or more) are classified according to their percentage-point decrease in Democratic vote between 1868 and 1872. The average per cent of Negroes in the potential voting population of the counties in each group is contained in column 3. The Table indicates rather conclusively that the enfranchisement of a large colored population in 1872 helped transmute Kentucky into a two-party state.

As a result, the Inner Bluegrass, though inclined Democratic, was narrowly divided between the two parties after 1872. Fayette county, at the very heart of the Bluegrass and with a colored population which was 47 per cent of the total in 1870, cast its lot more often with the Republicans than the Democrats between 1872 and 1932. Christian county, in the Penny-royal section and with a colored population 42 per cent of the total in 1870, likewise remained loyal to the Republican party in Presidential elections until 1932. Similar sections in the deep South have been Democratic strongholds since the Civil War, because of restrictions on the franchise imposed on the colored population.

No serious attempt has been made in Kentucky to deprive the Negro of the suffrage. The reasons for the more "enlightened" approach of Kentucky to Negro suffrage are two: 1) The Negro has never posed a serious challenge to white rule in the state. In 1870, the Negroes represented 17 per cent of the total population of the state, and in 1950 only 7 per cent. 2) Many political leaders recognized the potential value which such a large docile group represented as a lever to power, and took pains to protect their right to vote.

Therefore, the important political changes produced by the Civil War in Kentucky were two: 1) the ex-slaveholders tended to become Democrats; and 2) the former slaves became Republicans. The net result was to make of Kentucky a Democratic stronghold, but within a two-party political structure.

The state remained predominantly Democratic from the Civil War until the Populist period in the last decade of the nineteenth century, which witnessed a sharp decline in "normal" Democratic majorities in the state. The impact of Populism was pronounced on the vote of the metropolitan and coal counties of the state. Prior to 1896, the business leaders of the state

FIGURE 10

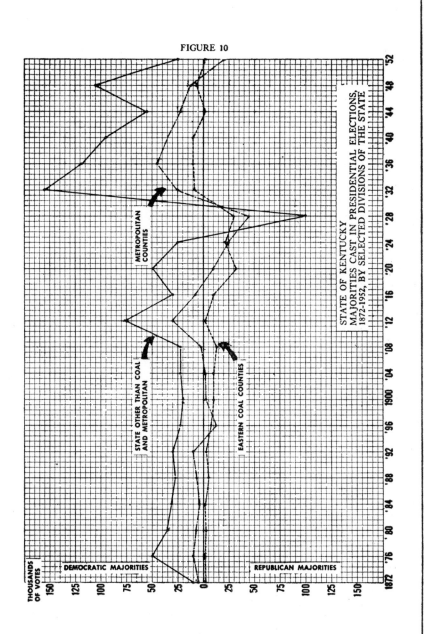

STATE OF KENTUCKY
MAJORITIES CAST IN PRESIDENTIAL ELECTIONS,
1872-1952, BY SELECTED DIVISIONS OF THE STATE

were, in large part, Democratically inclined. However, when the Democrats embraced Populism in 1896, the business community turned to the Republican party to repel this red-tinged threat to the "American way of life." Outside the coal and metropolitan counties Populism had little enduring effect on the political predispositions of the voters. The Southcentral Knobs region represents the single important exception to this generalization. Many of the Southcentral Knobs counties date their affiliation to the Republican faith from the Populist period. Populism as an issue was not primarily responsible for the plus Republican change that occurred in the area after 1896. The importance of the Populist period lay in the opportunity it afforded local Republican leaders to obtain control of the county governments. The business community was generous with its campaign contributions, designed to assure the defeat of Populist candidates. Republican leaders in the Knobs region, however, used the money both to assure majorities for anti-Populist candidates and to secure control of local offices. The nature of the continuing political change that has occurred in the Southcentral Knobs region is discussed in detail later in this chapter.

After 1896 and until the Great Depression, the three most important facts of Kentucky's political life were: 1) the increased strength of the Republican party in the urban and coal centers of the state after the election of 1896; 2) the increased population in the Eastern Coal counties and the urban centers and a resultant increase in the proportion of the state's total vote cast by them (in 1896 the vote of the four metropolitan counties of Jefferson, Kenton, Campbell, and

Boyd, plus the vote of the Eastern Coal counties represented only 23 per cent of the state's total vote cast, whereas in 1952 it constituted 42 per cent of the total) ; 3) the relative stability of the vote cast by the state outside the metropolitan and coal counties, both in terms of total vote and proportion cast for the two major parties.[1]

Figure 10 shows graphically the process by which these three factors helped make Kentucky an increasingly doubtful state politically after 1896. As indicated by the figure, the Eastern Coal counties' Republican majority gradually increased from approximately 2,000 votes immediately following the Civil War, to more than 30,000 votes in 1920. At the same time, the metropolitan counties of Jefferson, Kenton, Campbell, and Boyd also showed an increasing tendency to vote Republican, despite occasional oscillations in their vote, while both the proportionate division and the total vote cast remained almost constant in the remainder of the state. The net result, prior to 1932, was a secular downward trend in the "normal" Democratic majority in the state. As a result, the Republican party carried the state in the presidential elections of 1924 and 1928.

In 1928, the prospects for the Democratic party in Kentucky must have seemed dim indeed. In that year the Republican party carried the state by an unprecedented plurality and trends indicated that the future held in prospect increasing Republican strength. The Republican coal and urban counties' populations continued to increase while the potential vote of the remainder of the state remained relatively constant.

[1] See footnote on page 47.

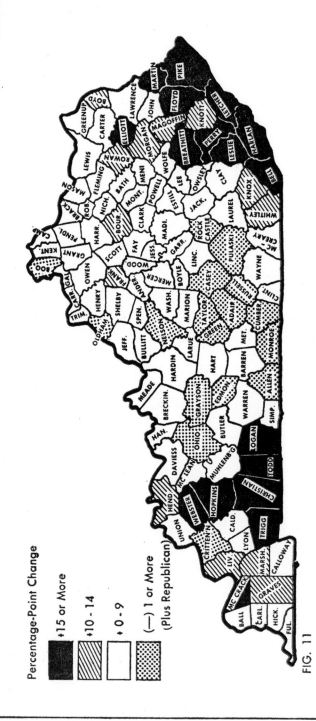

Percentage-Point Change

■ +15 or More

▨ +10 - 14

□ + 0 - 9

▒ (—) 1 or More
(Plus Republican)

FIG. 11

Political Change [1]

Percentage-Point Change in Democratic Percent of Two-Party Vote.   Presidential Elections 1916-1952.

1. Political change for the period 1916-1952 is measured by computing a line of regression (or secular trend line) for each of the counties of the state.   Consequently, the measure of change is a product of all the elections of the series and not the first and last elections.

Depression and Political Change

The Great Depression and the subsequent New Deal sharply reversed Kentucky's plus Republican trend and rendered the state, at least temporarily, safe once again for the Democratic party. Comparison of Figures 11 and 12 suggests that the resurgence of Democratic strength in the state was due, in large part, to the reaction of two elements of Kentucky's population to the New Deal and the depression: 1) the coal miners; and 2) the colored people. In addition, the figures indicate that the people of the low income counties of the state are tending to cast an increasing proportion of their vote for the Republican party.

In summary, only 25 per cent or 30 of the state's 120 counties are identified in Figure 11 as having experienced plus Democratic change of ten percentage-points or more and only 14 per cent or 17 counties registered plus Republican change over the period 1916-1952. During the same period, 87 per cent of the state's most important coal producing counties and 57 per cent of the counties with large colored populations registered plus Democratic gains of 10 percentage-points or more; and 59 per cent of the state's poorest counties experienced plus Republican change. We turn now to an analysis of the factors responsible for the political change that has occurred in these three classifications of counties.

1. The Coal Counties

The primary causal factors responsible for the revolutionary political change which has taken place in Kentucky's coal counties are four in number: 1) population change and the character of that change; 2) depression, New Deal legislation, and the growth of the labor movement; 3) political organization; and 4) culture change.

Development of Kentucky's Eastern Coal section did not take place until the first part of the twentieth century. Accompanying its development was a population growth of mushroom proportions. The Western Coal fields were exploited prior to the Eastern Coal section, but their relative importance has declined in recent years. Hopkins county alone, of the Western Coal counties has maintained a steady growth in both the production of coal and population. The remaining counties of the section, excepting Muhlenberg, have suffered a population decline since 1900 and Muhlenberg's population has declined since 1940. Therefore, plus Democratic change has not been as pronounced in the Western Coal fields as in the Eastern, outside Hopkins and Muhlenberg counties. The important fact about the population increase that has taken place in the coal counties is that it has been qualitative as well as quantitative. In Harlan county, for example, there were few people engaged in mining in 1900, whereas in 1950, 58 per cent of the employed population was occupied in producing 10,000,000 tons of coal.

It was at the time of the Great Depression that the coal counties experienced the political upheaval that, in many of them, placed the Democratic party in the position of majority party. It is inexact, however, to say that the depression "caused" the change that occurred. It is more accurate to say that the depression and the events that accompanied it released elements which were inherent in the socio-economic situation.

FIG. 12

Selected Characteristics of the Population by Counties, 1950.

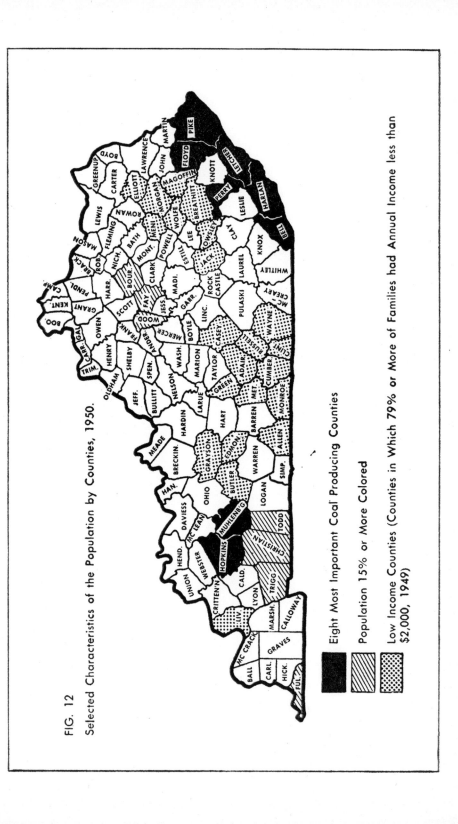

Eight Most Important Coal Producing Counties

Population 15% or More Colored

Low Income Counties (Counties in Which 79% or More of Families had Annual Income less than $2,000, 1949)

Plus Democratic change occurred in 1932 in the coal counties as it did elsewhere in the state and nation because of dissatisfaction with the party in power. However, the change not only endured in the coal counties, but was actually augmented or sustained in 1936, 1940 and 1948, when elsewhere the trend was back to a pre-1932 division between the parties.

The plus Democratic change in the coal counties endured, first, because the temporary dissatisfaction with the party in power was translated into permanent political strength by effective organization; and, secondly, because a considerable segment of the swollen population was inclined Democratic prior to the depression, but was restrained from giving this tendency expression by the tight control over the counties' political machinery exercised by the mine operators and the ruling families of the mountain counties. Veterans of the political wars in this section testify that the result of an election prior to 1932 approximated more closely a pleasant guessing game among like-minded people than a careful accounting of the wishes of the sovereign citizen. It was felt that counting the ballots represented a waste of time that might better be spent wresting coal from the bowels of the earth.

It was the United Mine Workers that consolidated the revolution of 1932. If the U.M.W. had not succeeded in its organizational efforts in the 1930's, it is probable that the political complexion of the coal counties would have reverted to something approaching its pre-New Deal status. But with unionization a pressure organization existed that challenged and to some extent supplanted the influence the operators enjoyed over the results of elections. Thereafter, instead of being "instructed" by their foremen as to the "right" way to vote, the miners were "advised" by Union officials as to the direction in which their self-interest might lie.

Culture change is another factor which is partially responsible for the coal region's plus Democratic change. Culture change is peculiarly unsusceptible to examination and measurement as a factor in political change, but its influence in the mountain counties has been substantial. The development of the mines has brought new people to the mountains; people with new ideas, new beliefs, new wants. Along with these people have come roads and railroads, police and law enforcement. In late years many of the children of the more well-to-do mountain people have left the hills at age eighteen to attend the University of Kentucky and other schools. At the University these students have been exposed to new ideas, and those who have returned have jolted the conservatism of their mountain brethren.

Therefore, the political change that has occurred in the mountain counties cannot be ascribed to any single factor, but is the product of a whole matrix of causes and effects interacting one with the other. The basic reason for the change, however, is the fact that the region was opened up by railroads and highways, and developed by the coal companies, bringing with that development population change, better communications with the outside world and wealth.

2. Counties with a Large Negro Population

Kentucky's colored voters enlisted their votes almost to a man on the side of Abraham Lincoln's Republican party following the Civil War. Elderly Negroes when reminiscing dwell at length on the debt the colored man owes the Republican party. Not only did its leader "fight a war for our freedom," but the Republicans were instrumental in safeguarding the right of the colored man to cast his vote.

The younger Negroes, however, look back to Franklin Roosevelt as a latter-day emancipator. They emphasize that the Republicans took the Negroes' vote for granted before 1932, and thank Franklin Roosevelt's Democratic party for lending a new value to the franchise by compelling the Republican party to compete for the colored vote. The changed orientation of the colored vote has had a considerable impact on political divisions in the old slave-holding Pennyroyal and Bluegrass sections, where the majority of the state's colored population is located.

The Pennyroyal, with the exception of Trigg county, was a Whig stronghold prior to the Civil War, ruling the state in company with the Bluegrass and with the cooperation of the mountain counties. Today the area has a higher percentage of Negroes than any other section of the Commonwealth and contains the county, Christian, with, proportionately, the largest Negro population. Bowling Green, county seat of Warren county, located in the Pennyroyal, was the Kentucky Confederate capital during the Civil War, and Christian county is the birthplace of Jefferson Davis.[1]

Post-Civil War political developments in Christian county are typical of Kentucky counties with a large Negro population. Since 1872, there has been a secu-

---

[1] Approximately two-hours ride from the monument marking Jeff Davis' birthplace is another park commemorating Abraham Lincoln's birthplace.

lar plus Democratic trend in the county, which has been accompanied by a secular downward trend in the percentage of the population which is colored. As has been noted elsewhere, the Negro in Kentucky has enjoyed the franchise without serious challenge since 1872 and has been inclined to vote Republican in overwhelming numbers until recently. Therefore, the decline in Negro population both percentagewise and absolutely has adversely affected the Republican vote in Christian county. Virtually every adult Negro moving out of Christian county prior to 1932 marked the leavetaking of a Republican vote. Since 1932, the plus Democratic change of the colored voters has helped accentuate the upward trend in the county's percentage Democratic vote, transforming the county from a Republican stronghold in presidential elections into a citadel of the Democratic party.[1]

Secondly, the socio-economic situation in Christian county made it extraordinarily difficult for the Republicans to maintain control. Most of the social and economic leaders of the community were and are inclined toward the Democratic party. It is to these leaders that most people must turn for favors, and particularly the Negroes. Consequently, the prolonged impact of the wishes of its economic leaders upon the political habits of the community were almost certain to produce an increase in the Democratic proportion of the vote. The county judge of Christian county attributes the switch from Republican to Democratic

---

[1] This is not as contradictory as it may seem. Even though there has been a plus Democratic shift of the rural Negro vote, it still remains primarily Republican by affiliation. Therefore, the Democrats gain both by emigration of the Negro and by his plus Democratic shift.

in local elections to the fact that the Republicans were without "qualified candidates."

The strongly Democratic sister Pennyroyal counties of Todd, Trigg and Logan have experienced a population and political change among Negroes similar to Christian's which has helped produce the plus Democratic change of these counties. In these three counties, however, the existence of strong Democratic organizations that have ruled without challenge since at least the turn of the century is also a factor in the plus Democratic change that has occurred.

The effect of a strong organization which maintains power over a considerable period of time is to make believers out of all but the most stout-of-heart. There are many reasons why great political power only half sensibly used begets even greater power. When a person in such a community has a brush with the law his fate is decided by the political authorities. If he feels that his property assessment is too high he must plead with the political authorities for "justice." When he wants a road repaired or built or a job with the state or county, or snow cleared from a road, he must go to the political authorities who are also representatives of the machine. Therefore, good judgment usually demands support of the machine in its occasional political battles. This support is not very painful to give, for the alternatives are seldom better and often worse. Thus as more and more of the minority group conform to the dominant political value, the result is a long-term accretion in the strength of the dominant political group.

A final and very important part of the explanation for the Pennyroyal's plus Democratic change is general

satisfaction with New Deal policies. Since the late
nineteenth century, western Kentucky has tended to
support "liberal" Democrats in an effort to obtain
remedial farm legislation. Under the New Deal many
western Kentuckians feel that their aspirations have
been realized. Therefore, the general reaction to the
New Deal has been favorable. Many of the more
direct benefits of New Deal measures have been felt
in this area. Kentucky Lake, a Tennessee Valley
Authority reservoir, borders Trigg county. T.V.A. has
brought recreation and industrial development to the
area. Because of T.V.A. and Alben Barkley, the
Atomic Energy Commission has constructed a large
plant at Paducah, providing high paying jobs for many
residents of the section.

Thus the plus Democratic change in the Pennyroyal
section is attributable to many factors. Population
change and the Negro vote is an important ingredient
in the change that has occurred. However, it is doubtful if the change would have been pronounced and
widespread if the twin factors of strong Democratic
organization and general satisfaction with Democratic
policies had not also been present.

The Inner Bluegrass, like the Pennyroyal, has a
large percentage of Negroes in its population, but unlike the Pennyroyal there has not been a shift *in toto*
of the electorate's expressions of party preference in
favor of Democratic party candidates. There are three
significant factors differentiating the Bluegrass counties with large colored populations from the Pennyroyal counties. These are: 1) the Inner Bluegrass
counties have relatively large urban populations (and
labor unions are weak); 2) as a complement to

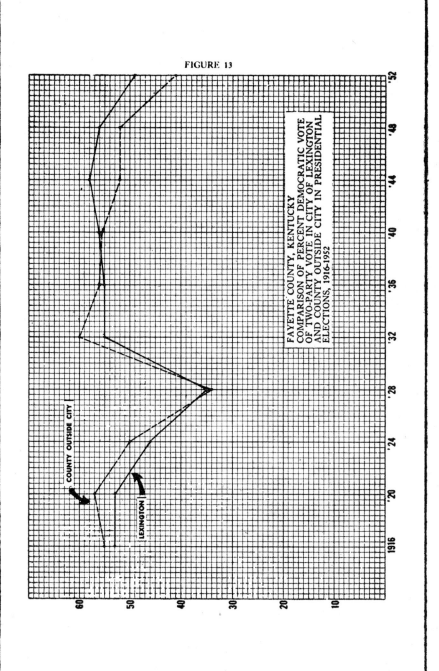

FIGURE 13

FAYETTE COUNTY, KENTUCKY
COMPARISON OF PERCENT DEMOCRATIC VOTE
OF TWO-PARTY VOTE IN CITY OF LEXINGTON
AND COUNTY OUTSIDE CITY IN PRESIDENTIAL
ELECTIONS, 1916-1952

COUNTY OUTSIDE CITY

LEXINGTON

urbanization a substantial suburban populace has come into being; 3) the farmers of the Bluegrass are of a different stripe from those of the Pennyroyal and Jackson Purchase. Many of the Bluegrass landowners are gentleman farmers who have purchased land as a form of conspicuous waste. Therefore, there is not the same interest in "liberal" farm policies as exists in the Pennyroyal where the land is the source of the daily bread.

The Bluegrass counties have almost invariably supported "conservative" candidates and policies. The section is a center of the state's wealth and its social and economic leaders are often referred to as "Bourbons." The New Deal by its very nature lacked appeal to the leaders of the Bluegrass. Therefore, unlike the Pennyroyal, the plus Democratic shift in the vote of the colored population and the leavetaking of colored people from the more rural sections of the Inner Bluegrass has been balanced by the tendency of other elements in the population to vote Republican because of their disapproval of New Deal measures.

Figure 13 provides visual evidence of this compensatory shift. The figure traces the percentage Democratic vote in the Bluegrass city of Lexington and the county outside the city, from 1916 to 1952. As the graph indicates, the county outside the city tended to vote more Democratic than did the city until 1936, from which date the city has voted more Democratic than the county. Democratic leaders say, "We used to feel confident if the Republicans carried the city by only a narrow margin, but now the situation is reversed." One Republican observed that "we have traded the Negroes for the suburban vote, a trade that is eminently satisfactory to us." The net result is a stand-off, despite Democratic gains immediately following the depression. The long-term trends, however, would seem to indicate that the Democrats have suffered the worst of the bargain. This is indicated because the proportion that the county vote represents of the total vote is increasing. In the 1954 local elections in Fayette county, the Republican party succeeded in electing a full slate of candidates in the county for the first time since the Roosevelt revolution.

An additional factor in the political spectrum of the Bluegrass counties is the character of the post-depression population influx experienced by them. Mrs. T. E. Van Meter, head of a settlement house located in a slum district of Lexington popularly known as "Irishtown," testifies that it is difficult to find an Irishman in Irishtown. According to Mrs. Van Meter, most of the occupants of Irishtown in 1955 were blonde-haired Anglo-Saxons whose roots are in Kentucky's Republican eastern mountains. The erstwhile Democratically-inclined Irish had long since deserted "Irishtown," testifies that it is difficult to find an at the edge of town, pondering the price of inflation. Thus the long-term outlook for the Bluegrass would seem to be an increasing Republican vote.

3. The Low Income Counties

The visitor to Kentucky's Southcentral Knobs region sometimes has the feeling that he has entered the world made famous by Al Capp. Rude log cabins are seen perched precariously on hillsides, surrounded by tobacco, corn (planted by some alchemy on the precipitous hillsides), and swarms of children. This section of Kentucky is the state's least wealthy by almost any criterion. The per capita income is the lowest, and the case rate of people receiving public assistance is the highest; on an isolation scale involving such items as roads, telephones, newspapers, and radios, the section is the most isolated in the state.[1]

The Knobs people are fundamentally the same as those living in more favored sections. The interiors of their cabins are as neat and as attractive as their means permit. They are suspicious of strangers, but generous to a fault with their friends. They are a proud people. They are proud of the traditions of independence and self-sufficiency long associated with the hill character, and with which their political leaders regale them in Fourth of July oratory. And they feel that recent events have tended to undermine the old and the "good" way of life.

Franklin Delano Roosevelt and his New Deal is the whipping boy on whom many of the frustrations of the area are released. The New Deal farm program and public assistance programs, along with such depression measures as W.P.A., are blamed for many of the economic and social ills of the region. "Shiftlessness" on the part of some inhabitants is ascribed to New Deal "give-away" measures. In turn, these measures are said to have vitiated the traditional independence and self-reliance of the hill folk. Finally, it is the opinion of many Knobs people that most New Deal programs helped the large landowner and the urban organized laboring man infinitely more than the subsistence farmer. The important fact, however,

---

[1] Based upon research performed by Department of Rural Sociology, University of Kentucky.

is that many of the people of the region feel a strong dislike for the New Deal and all its works, and that this feeling has been translated into increased Republican strength at the ballot box, as shown by Figure 11.

Kentuckians, when asked, find the plus Republican trend of the Knobs section difficult to explain. Those natives of the area who give the matter any thought usually cite as the reason the influence of some opinion leader, such as an M.D. or a great landowner. On the other hand, one prominent Democratic politician observed, "Hell, we've just gerrymandered that section and forgotten about it! That's the reason it's more Republican. If we made an effort we could swing it in our direction, but it isn't worth it. It's poor, isolated, and the population isn't great and is declining." It is interesting that few rationales advanced by residents were based upon the political opinions of the populace or upon population change. However, as in other sections of the state where important political change has occurred, these two factors are of compelling importance in the political change that has occurred in the section.

In order to understand the influence of population change on the plus Republican trend in the area it is necessary to see it in terms of two dimensions. In the first place, because it is poverty-stricken, the Southcentral Knobs exports a large percentage of its population. It is part of what Odum called the "seed bed of the nation." Families are large and the land is poor.

South of the Southcentral Knobs section is Tennessee. The section of Tennessee that borders on the Southcentral Knobs is similar to the Knobs in numerous respects. It is poverty-stricken and it is also part of the "seed bed of the nation." In 1870 it differed from the Knobs in only one important respect. The Tennessee hill country was and is one-sidedly Republican, whereas much of the Knobs section was inclined toward the Democratic party.

Significantly, the population flow from both the Tennessee hills and the Kentucky Knobs region has been northward. Therefore, very few of the Southcentral Knobs people may be found in the Tennessee hills. However, many of the Tennessee hill people have settled in the Knobs. For example, in 1870 Tennesseans represented approximately 50 per cent of the population residing in the Southcentral Knobs counties which was born outside the state.[1] Therefore, through the decades since 1870 the tendency in the Southcentral Knobs region has been to receive a population which is more heavily weighted in favor of the Republican party than is the population leaving the area. Thus the poverty of the Knobs section has played an important part in the type of population movement experienced by it. Poverty has encouraged migration of the native population and discouraged in-migration from any area other than the equally impoverished Tennessee hills.

Therefore, poverty is the warp and the woof of the political change that has occurred in the Knobs section. The poverty of the region has produced a type of population influx calculated to increase the per-

---

[1] In 1870, of 11,654 people residing in the ten southcentral Kentucky counties which experienced a plus Republican trend and born outside the state, 5,955 or 51 per cent were born in Tennessee. Twenty per cent of the state's population born outside the state was born in Tennessee in 1870. Source: *United States Census, 1870.*

centage Republican vote of the region, and through the cultural insolation engendered by it has insulated the section from the impact of events such as the Great Depression and the growth of the labor movement. Because the Knobs did not suffer greatly from the depression (they were already poor), the people do not identify the Republican party with economic disaster. On the contrary, it is common to hear an old timer say, "Why, during the depression I could take a dozen eggs to the store and get in return goods worth $2.00. Today, they give me 30 cents for the dozen eggs, and make me pay $2.00 for the same goods." Therefore, the Democratic party is blamed for inflation in the section and is given little or no credit for restoring prosperity, because, as a matter of fact, there is no prosperity.

Conclusions

The Civil War, the Populist period, and the Great Depression are the three key points in the history of Kentucky politics in terms of political change. The Civil War made Democrats of the Bourbon Whigs and transmuted Kentucky into a Democratic stronghold from a center of Whiggery. The state remained dominantly Democratic until the Populist period. The tendency of the Democratic party to champion economic and social nostrums at the turn of the century alienated many Bourbons and business leaders from the party. Thereafter and until 1932, the state was marginal politically.

The Great Depression and the New Deal, by creating conditions making possible a change in the power structure of the coal counties, released the Democratic potential of the vote from that section. In addition, the about face of the Negro vote and the favorable reaction to the New Deal in western Kentucky produced Democratic gains. The result was the return of Kentucky to the ranks of the "safely" Democratic states.

Since 1932, the urban counties and the state outside the urban and coal counties have shown a tendency to return to the political posture assumed by them prior to 1932. The coal counties, though, have seemingly achieved a new equilibrium between the two political parties, leaving them narrowly divided *in toto,* but with the Democratic party faring better than was the case prior to 1932. In terms of recent political developments, therefore, the coal counties represent the single most important reason for the continuing strength of the Democratic party in the state, as was demonstrated by Kentucky's failure to join the nation in the Eisenhower landslide of 1952. In 1952, the division in the state outside the urban and coal counties left the Democratic forces with a majority of approximately 20,000 votes, as had so often been the case between 1896 and 1932. The Republicans emerged triumphant in the metropolitan counties by a margin of some 15,000 votes. By pre-1932 standards this division would have heralded Republican victory. However, the Democratic vote in the coal counties was but little affected by the Eisenhower landslide, and Adlai Stevenson carried the state by the very narrowest of margins. In 1956, however, the tremendous Eisenhower vote in the cities carried the state for him.

If existing trends in the state continue unchecked, the prospects are that the state will assume, once again, a marginal political complexion. The urban counties represent the only localities in the state wherein the population is increasing. Unfortunately for the Democrats, the political trend in the urban counties is in a plus Republican direction, whereas the division between the two major parties elsewhere in the state has, seemingly, achieved a new equilibrium. The principal reason for the decline in Democratic strength in Kentucky's urban areas is the weakness of organized labor. The cities of Kentucky contain relatively small diversified industries and the unions never succeeded in making permanent the Roosevelt revolution by organizing these industries. The 1956 Eisenhower victory in Kentucky, along with that of the two Republican candidates for Senator, tends to substantiate this contention.

The character of the long-term voting trends in Kentucky helps shed light on the mechanics of political change. Environmental change of a radical nature seems to be a pre-condition of pronounced and durable political change, judging from the nature of political change in Kentucky. Population change is the most common type of environmental change which makes possible enduring political change. However, during critical junctures in the history of the nation, such as the Civil War and the Great Depression, environmental changes have occurred independent of population change which have been great enough to induce pronounced political change. Unionization and the emancipation of the slaves are good examples of this type of environmental change.

Political organization, individual leadership, and the policies of the great parties are important as precipitants and preservatives of political change. However, they rarely, if ever, are capable of producing long-term change independent of some basic change in the political environment.

CHAPTER IV

WEST VIRGINIA — A MULTI-PARTY STATE

FROM 1940 until 1956, West Virginia had four primary political groupings, mainly: 1) the United
Mine Workers, labor, or "liberals"; 2) the Bourbons,
rural or "conservative" Democrats; 3) the Statehouse
or Neely-Hanna faction of the Democratic party; and
4) the Republican party. In terms of the two-party
system, the coal miners, Bourbons, and Statehouse
people were all Democrats. However, the contests between labor, the Bourbons, and the Statehouse faction
for control of the state's Democratic party decided the
question, "Who shall rule?" What follows is both a
chronicle of the factional conflicts within the state's
Democratic party and an analysis of the consequences
in terms of party structure and organization. The
analysis is in terms of the pre-1956 period. However,
subsequent events, such as the Republican victory in
the 1956 gubernatorial election, have not changed the
nature of the fundamental political division within the
state.

Political Organization in West Virginia

In 1955, most West Virginians, if asked to name the
state's principal political figures, would have nominated Senator Matthew M. Neely, an ageless veteran
of West Virginia politics; Homer Hanna, Clerk of the
Federal Court in Charleston and owner of an insurance agency; Walter Hallanan, Republican National
Committeeman from West Virginia and President of
the Plymouth Oil Company; and William Blizzard,

President of District 17, United Mine Workers. During the periodic political convulsions that upset and excited the partisans of the state at the time, speculation centered upon the political activities of these four men.

In 1940 Matt Neely ended Bourbon rule of the state and the Democratic party. Thereby, he assumed a dominant position in the state's political hierarchy. Neely retired from the United States Senate in order to contest the 1940 Democratic gubernatorial nomination with the Bourbon candidate. Neely's success was due to two factors: 1) the United Mine Workers' leaders were incensed at the efforts of the incumbent Bourbon Democratic governor to, as they saw it, destroy the union. Therefore, the union leaders happily supported Neely in the primary; 2) Neely was not identified with the United Mine Workers, but enjoyed a following which extended into every geographic, economic, and cultural segment of the state. Most contemporary observers agreed that Neely was not a "liberal" man. Instead, they felt that he simply used a tool to power in 1940, in the same fashion as politicians of 1896 used the tool of capitalist power to seize political control.

The election of Matt Neely as governor in 1940 marked the birth of the so-called Statehouse or Neely-Hanna faction of the Democratic party. The term "Statehouse" has the same meaning in West Virginia as "Administration" in Kentucky. It designates the people who control the state's patronage and contracts. The names of Matt Neely and Homer Hanna were commonly associated with the term Statehouse, because it was felt that they exercised decisive authority in the government of the state.

Neely's authority in the Statehouse group derived from the fact that he molded and created it. He hand-picked his successor, Clarence Meadows, as governor, and had a commanding voice in the selection of suc-ceeding Statehouse candidates for major office. In addition, he was the "grand old man" of the state's Democratic party. Therefore, most powerful State-house people looked to Neely for leadership. However, his power was not absolute in the state. The governor often made independent decisions contrary to Neely's wishes. The governor knew, though, that the penalty for too many such decisions was likely to be political death.

Observers saw Homer Hanna's role in the State-house organization as that of both a "political adviser" and "political boss." Many looked upon him as a wily Richelieu dangling the puppets of government by strong cords. Mr. Hanna depreciated his role in state government, contending that he could be called no more than a good friend of the governor, a friend who was occasionally called upon to provide political advice and counsel.[1] Bill Blizzard, U.M.W. executive, claims Hanna as a protege. During the depression Hanna was fired from a W.P.A. job for the use of funds for political purposes. Blizzard thereupon appointed him to a U.M.W. position. In 1940, Blizzard recommended Hanna to Neely as Democratic campaign manager.

---

[1] In the course of a two-hour interview with Mr. Hanna, the Federal Court Clerk, he was called by 1) the governor who asked advice concerning the proper way to handle a Democratic county leader who was causing the governor some concern, 2) the head, Department of Labor, who sought advice concerning an appointment, 3) the administrative assistant to Senator Kilgore who requested an appointment.

He was so successful as campaign manager that Neely
never permitted him to return to his U.M.W. post.
After 1940, he came to be identified, along with Neely,
as a leader of the Statehouse faction. Like Neely, his
contacts reached into every stratum of West Virginia
society. Bankers and union people alike regarded him
as "sound," and listened to his proposals with respect.

Formally, the only government post held by Hanna
was that of clerk of the Federal Court in Charleston.
His business was insurance; a remunerative pursuit
for Hanna for he received a large share of the state's
insurance business. As Statehouse people said, "The
price of his insurance is no greater than others charge,
why shouldn't we buy it from him?"

Hanna's power could not be measured by the positions he held, or by the precincts he controlled. His
power was a product of his personality. His friends
and enemies testify that he is likeable. He makes you
feel important, and will give you an hour or six hours
of his time. He sincerely likes people, and enjoys talk-
ing to them. Because of these character traits, he has
been successful in politics, and because of his success
he came to the attention of men such as Blizzard and
Neely.

Thus the Statehouse group had three levels of leadership. First, there was Neely, the "grand old man" of
Democratic politics and the acknowledged boss, then
Hanna, the tactician and strategist, and, finally, the
governor, the lieutenant in charge of field operations.

William Blizzard, President, District 17, United
Mine Workers of America, is a powerful political figure
in West Virginia. His District includes the coal coun-

ties of southern West Virginia and is the largest in the union. Mr. Blizzard's place in the spectrum of the West Virginia political scene may be most fully appreciated through a description of a telephone conversation between him and a Democratic official. The Democratic official in question was, in 1954, state publicity director and a member of the State Unemployment Compensation Board which adjudicates disputes concerning the payment of unemployment compensation claims.

The Democratic official called Bill Blizzard to request that a membership list of District 17 members be provided him for circularization purposes. Mr. Blizzard's reply consisted, first of all, in an attack upon the official and the board of which he was a member for some of its decisions. Mr. Blizzard felt that the board had been unduly legalistic in deciding against some claims for unemployment compensation on the part of the U.M.W. members. Finally Mr. Blizzard informed the official that the rules of the U.M.W. forbade giving anyone such a list. However, in a more pleasant tone of voice, he added that if the official would send him the material that he would distribute it to his membership.

As the telephone conversation indicates, the United Mine Workers union is not and never has been a part of the Democratic organization of the state. It is a separate and distinct interest group. However, because it customarily supports Democratic candidates it has special claims on Democratic officials and presses those claims with vigor. It is, in the classic sense, a powerful interest group which seeks special privileges for its members. Political leaders who rely upon business support for nomination and election engage in similar telephone calls with business leaders.

Homer Hanna compares the organization of West Virginia's pre-1956 Democratic party with that of a church. In terms of Hanna's analogy, Senator Neely was the party's pope, Homer Hanna the papal nuncio, and the governor the bishop. The monsignor of each county was the "Statehouse man," the West Virginia equivalent of Kentucky's "Administration man." In West Virginia, the Statehouse man was often the Democratic county chairman or the sheriff, but not invariably. The most important considerations in the appointment of Statehouse men were the real power of the individual and his loyalty to the Statehouse group. Continuing the analogy, the parish priests of the organization were the precinct leaders.

The cement that held the Statehouse organization together was patronage, contracts, highways and parks. The single factor absent in the analogy is common devotion to an idea. This ingredient was supplied in only one sector of the organization. Many of the political leaders among the coal miners are genuinely devoted to the idea that political organization provides the key to the betterment of the lot of submerged groups. Some of these people are unselfish in their political motivations. In the main, however, the organization people had only the cement of political preferment to bind them to the Statehouse group.

In most counties the Statehouse group had five categories of people who worked for it in the primaries and on general election day. These categories are: 1) the state employees, mainly highway and liquor store employees; 2) businessmen and other favored parties who contracted with the state for the delivery of goods or services; 3) people such as liquor agents who retained their jobs with private companies on sufferance of the Statehouse group; 4) interest groups which were often allied with the machine, such as the United Mine Workers and school teachers; and 5) county courthouse people who in some cases worked with the Statehouse group, depending upon arrangements concerning such items as patronage and parks.

The Statehouse group as an independent entity was strongest in the Republican counties. The strength of the Statehouse faction in Republican counties was due to the absence of competition from a Democratic county courthouse faction, as in Kentucky. The Democratic partisans in Republican counties must turn to the state for patronage and contracts, because the Republicans possess the local emoluments of power. Therefore, in these counties the machinery of party government was in the hands of Statehouse people.

The Statehouse group, in general, enjoyed the support of the U.M.W. Therefore, it was usually able to depend upon the coal counties for overwhelming majorities for its candidates in the primaries and general elections. The Statehouse people attempted to make the coal county political leaders at the local level more party conscious than union conscious. This effort was partially successful. However, the U.M.W. never lost its dominant political position in the coal counties.

The conservative rural Democratic counties of southern and eastern West Virginia ordinarily returned majorities for primary opponents of Statehouse candidates. The political leaders of the rural Democratic counties ruled the party prior to 1940 and not unnaturally would have liked to reassert their authority. However, the patronage and contract power of the governor was strong enough to reduce the anti-Statehouse majorities in the Bourbon counties to a safe level, if the Statehouse candidate was not overly obnoxious to local opinion.

Because the Republican party was out of power before 1956, its organization was substantially different from that of the Democratic party. Each county organization was relatively independent with few strong patronage or contract ties to a central organization.

In spite of this anarchic situation, Walter Hallanan managed to provide the party with strong leadership. The cement that bound the local organizations to Hallanan had three ingredients: 1) he controlled most of the federal patronage dispensed to Republicans in the state; 2) he expended a goodly quantity of his time and his private fortune on the development of a strong organization; 3) his personality is similar to that of Homer Hanna's. He is likeable. He is dependable.

Hallanan's personal power stemmed from four sources: 1) his personal friendships with county leaders; 2) his friendly relations with coal operators, businessmen, and Bill Blizzard of the U.M.W.; 3) his friendship with Neely and other Democratic leaders; and 4) the possession of a private fortune giving him unlimited time and resources to devote to politics.

The novelist might find something sinister in all these relationships. On the contrary, though, they were most simple and direct. In most Republican statewide primaries, Hallanan backed a candidate. In some cases the candidate was "his" man. In other instances he was forced to choose between several objectionable alternatives. In any event, after making a choice he sought support for his man. In the pursuit of this objective, he visited every county of the state and talked to local leaders. A good example of the type of exchange that occurred on these trips is the time in 1942 he approached "Cap" Ferguson, the Charleston Negro political leader and a "Hallanan man," in an effort to secure support for Revercomb in opposition to Funkhouser in the Republican senatorial primary. The two shook hands, exchanged pleasantries, discussed the local political situation, and finally Hallanan said, " 'Cap', I wish you'd back Revercomb in the primary." Ferguson, though a Hallanan man, had already pledged his support to Funkhouser. Therefore, he was forced to reply: "Mr. Hallanan, I met Mr. Funkhouser last week and was impressed by him. I think that Funkhouser would make the better candidate so I promised him my support. I didn't know at that time that you were supporting Revercomb." Hallanan did not get upset or angry because of the unexpected reversal. He took the bad news in stride and parted on the best of terms with "Cap." The next time Hallanan approached Mr. Ferguson, the Negro leader was able to support his man.

A few years after Hallanan's disappointment, Funkhouser approached Ferguson for support in a situation the reverse of the first. This time Ferguson was pledged to Funkhouser's opponent. Upon being informed of this lamentable fact, Funkhouser became furious and charged Ferguson with bad faith. The good Mr. Funkhouser thereby succeeded in losing Ferguson's support for life instead of for one election.

It is not surprising that Walter Hallanan, national committeeman from West Virginia, political leader, and millionaire president of Plymouth Oil Company had close relations with the state's business leaders. After 1928, the coal and industrial Kanawha River Valley counties represented the core of Hallanan's strength. He relied primarily on these counties for the votes necessary to nominate "his" candidates in Republican primaries.

It is surprising, perhaps, that Hallanan retained control over the southern industrial and coal counties in Republican primaries after the 1932 New Deal revolution. The explanation for Hallanan's continued success in this section is two-sided. In the first place, he enjoyed political power in West Virginia's coal counties for the same reason that the Statehouse group controlled the state's Republican counties. The coal county Republicans were without local offices and contracts to gladden the hearts of party stalwarts. Therefore, Hallanan was the only source of jobs for the faithful and funds for the conduct of campaigns after the Democratic avalanche of 1932. Consequently, Hallanan's suggestions as to candidates were treated with more than ordinary respect by the Republican political leaders of the counties. This situation is, of course, different since the election of a Republican state administration in 1956.

In the second place, Walter Hallanan's relationships were very nearly as close with Blizzard, the U.M.W. leader, as with the operators. The relationship between

Hallanan and Blizzard was mutually profitable. Blizzard, at worst, did nothing to interfere with Hallanan's control of the Republican organization in the coal counties. Thereby, Hallanan's reserve of primary votes remained inviolate. In return, Blizzard had the nice insurance of friends on both sides of the political fence. The dividends which accrued to Blizzard included occasional Republican support for key U.M.W. backed legislative measures, and, according to many observers, the "political assassination" of unusually objectionable Republican candidates.

Hallanan's friendship with Democratic leaders rose from two political freshets: 1) mutual respect for fellow "pros"; and 2) the fact that Hallanan depended upon Democratic counties for much of the primary support received by his candidates, while the State-house people were equally dependent upon the vote of Republican counties in the Democratic primaries. By maintaining friendly relations, the Democratic and Republican leaders sustained one another's power, whereas cut-throat competition might have led to mutual destruction.

In Hancock county most of the political forces discussed in this chapter come to grips. The following case study of the political situation there in 1955 brings to life the preceding analysis of political organization in West Virginia.

Hancock county is at the northern extremity of West Virginia's northern panhandle. The county was Republican before 1932, but voted Democratic thereafter. Two industries are dominant in the county; steel-making and gambling. The town of Weirton, located in Hancock county, is a one-company town, dominated by the Weirton Steel Company.

Thomas E. Millsop was president of the Weirton Steel Company in 1955 as well as mayor of Weirton. Politically, Millsop was a sharp critic of Hallanan's leadership of the Republican party in West Virginia. In 1952, Millsop supported Eisenhower for the Republican nomination in opposition to Hallanan's support of Taft.

In 1955, many people spoke of a Millsop faction within West Virginia's Republican party. In reality, no such faction existed in state-wide form. Millsop possessed neither the time nor the necessary following to bring such a group into being. The split between Hallanan and Millsop was not a liberal-conservative schism. Millsop was at least as conservative as Hallanan. In the words of Weirton Steel's publicity director, "Millsop supported Eisenhower because he thought he could win."

Philip Hill, former chairman of the state's Citizens for Eisenhower organization, represented unorganized liberal Republican thought in the state. In 1952, Mr. Hill was a candidate for election as a delegate-at-large to the Republican National Convention. He was defeated, ranking sixth in a field of twelve. It is significant that Hill did not run well in the northern panhandle counties where Millsop, another Eisenhower supporter, received overwhelming majorities in his race for election as delegate from the First Congressional District. For example, in Hancock county where Millsop was strongest, Millsop received 3924 votes, ranking first among all candidates, and Hill received only 1498 votes, ranking sixth among the candidates for delegate-at-large. Needless to say, Mr. Hill did not wax enthusiastic at the mention of Millsop's name.

Millsop did not pretend to lead any substantial segment of the Republican party. In the northern panhandle section, he had the power to affect the results of local elections and primaries, but even in the northern panhandle, his power was far from absolute. In 1952, Hallanan-backed candidates for delegate-at-large pooled large votes in every county of the panhandle but Hancock. Thus Millsop ranked as a commanding figure only in Hancock county.

A visitor to Republican headquarters in Weirton during the 1954 campaign would probably have met Bill Huff if he had loitered long enough. Bill Huff was a machinist at Weirton Steel Corporation. Huff also had the distinction of being the man who organized the Weirton Independent Union. Finally, Huff was the president of the Weirton Republican Club.

A former secretary in the personnel department of Weirton Steel states that Huff never received pay for his political or union activities as such, although he was given liberal time off from his regular job to devote to these responsibilities. An additional compensation Huff did enjoy in his political and union work was the ear and friendship of the president of the company.

Another habitue of Republican headquarters was Weirton's Bill Tompos, a former business agent of the Carpenter's Union, and a defeated candidate for nomination to the House of Delegates on the Democratic ticket. Tompos devoted his attention to the cultivation of dissension within Democratic party ranks. He attended and promoted protest meetings at which the alleged tie-up between Hancock county gamblers and the Statehouse group was scored. The Republican county chairman was a schoolteacher who bubbled when he told of Millsop's generosity to the city. It seems that two country clubs had been built, several parks constructed, and "oh, so many things" done for the city as a result of philanthropic impulses on the part of Mr. Millsop, the Weirton Steel president. In view of the impulsive Millsop's generosity neither Mr. Millsop nor Mr. Huff nor the county chairman could understand why the unappreciative workers persisted in voting Democratic on election day.

On the Democratic side, the leader and Statehouse man was Dick Wright, an ex-sheriff and owner of a tourist court located directly across the Lincoln Highway from a gambling establishment.

Dick Wright's power was a many-sided affair. First, as Statehouse man in the county he had the patronage and contract authority which customarily accompanied such a position. Secondly, his patronage authority extended to such positions as that of steward at the Wheeling Downs racetrack. Thirdly, Wright was sheriff during the labor wars in Weirton. As sheriff, he had the delicate job of discouraging the union organizers who disturbed the tranquility of this smoggy Shangri-la. According to many of Weirton's citizens, Wright's anti-union activities during the thirties provided a bond between him and Millsop. Therefore, according to these people, Mr. Millsop, though unhappy about gambling and Democratic dominance

of the county, felt unable to take appropriate action
against the resourceful Dick Wright.

Bob Edwards, Chairman of the Hancock county
Democratic party, was unemployed in 1955, because
during the 1954 Democratic primary campaign Mr.
Edwards supported a candidate about whom Dick
Wright was unenthusiastic. As a result, Mr. Edwards
lost his job as deputy sheriff. In addition, Mr. Edwards lost a $50 per day job at Wheeling Downs race-
track. Not surprisingly, the unhappy Mr. Edwards
lost a good deal of his enthusiasm for the county's
Statehouse organization. In fact, he was transformed
into an advocate of political reform, and condemned
with great vigor and fine impartiality the time-honored,
according to Mr. Edwards, Hancock county custom
of rewarding deputy sheriffs for overlooking the existence of gambling establishments.

Social and Economic Divisions

The political organization of West Virginia's Democratic party consists of two main groupings in social
and economic terms; first, the people variously described as conservative, rural, or Bourbon; and, secondly, the United Mine Worker or labor faction of
the party.

The Bourbons ruled West Virginia's Democratic
party prior to 1940. Bourbon Democratic strength is
geographically concentrated in the southcentral portion of the state and extends from there along the
southern border of the state to its eastern tip. The 16
Bourbon Democratic counties [1] have three distinguish-
ing social and economic characteristics: 1) they rank

---

[1] Counties which supported winning candidate in three or more Democratic
gubernatorial primaries, 1924-1936.

(with only one exception) among the 27 counties of the state with a population more than one-third rural farm; 2) they count among their number four of the seven counties in which there were 1000 or more slaves in 1860; and 3) they include ten of the state's sixteen traditionally Democratic counties.[1]

The Bourbon Democrats ruled West Virginia from 1871 to 1896 and from 1932 to 1940. During this period they elected nine governors. Six of the nine Bourbon Democratic governors were from former important slaveholding areas of the state. By way of contrast, the Republican party has elected eleven governors, only three of whom hailed from once-great slaveholding counties.

The laboring people, particularly in the coal fields, rank as a second important economic group which calls itself Democratic. The United Mine Workers or "labor" faction of the party in coalition with the Neely-Hanna or Statehouse organization dominated the Democratic party from 1940 to 1956. The extent to which the state's Bourbon Democratic counties were frozen out of "their" party after 1940 is indicated by the fact that not one of the Bourbon counties can be counted among those which consistently supported the Neely-Hanna or winning candidates in Democratic primaries after 1940. The degree to which the new ruling coalition has been dependent upon U.M.W. support, on the other hand, is shown by the fact that thirteen of the fifteen consistently pro-Neely-Hanna counties[2] from 1940 to 1948 were strongly unionized coal

---

[1] Counties which voted Democratic in 19 of 21 presidential elections, 1872-1952.

[2] Counties carried by Neely-Hanna or winning candidate in every (7) Democratic gubernatorial and senatorial primary, 1940-48.

counties. Thus before 1940 the state's rural counties exercised a commanding voice in determining the identity of candidates for high office. After 1940 the coal counties largely determined the winners of Democratic primaries.

A third (non-economic) group within the Democratic party is the Neely-Hanna faction, or "the organization."[1] The organization's support is separable because the voters it controls are independent of the great social and economic groupings of the party. The organization's electoral support stems from its position astride the feed troughs of political preferment. As in Kentucky, the organization receives most of its support in Democratic primaries in the Republican counties. Eleven of the 20 organization[2] or Statehouse counties from 1944 to 1952 were strongly Republican, and six strongly Democratic (see figure 14 for definition of Democratic and Republican counties). Two of the six strongly Democratic counties counted among the "organization" counties were Hancock and Brooke in the northern panhandle. The Statehouse group's organization strength in the northern panhandle derived from its alliance with strong local leaders, such as Dick Wright of Hancock, and "understandings" with personages in the gambling world. The Statehouse group failed to carry the "organization" counties in 1940 because the Bourbons controlled the Statehouse and therefore possessed the "organizational strength" in these counties.

---

[1] Even though the Neely-Hanna group lost the Statehouse in 1956, the "organization" still exists. The identifying names change but the organization is immortal.

[2] Counties in which Neely-Hanna candidate did not receive plurality in 1940 when it was *not* the organization, but received plurality in all Democratic gubernatorial primaries, 1944-1952, when the Neely-Hanna faction succeeded the Bourbons as the organization.

The story of West Virginia politics since 1932 is largely a tale of the struggles for power between the three principal economic and organizational groups within the Democratic party. The Bourbon Democrats reaped the first harvests of the New Deal period, electing the Democratic governors of 1932 and 1936. William Guy Kump, Governor, 1932-1936, and Homer A. Holt, Governor, 1936-1940, never exhibited any enthusiasm for the New Deal. They were dilatory about accepting federal aid and were accused of the deliberate sabotage of many New Deal measures. Homer Holt was overtly anti-union. During his administration he embarked on a course of action which U.M.W. leaders construed as a deliberate effort to destroy the union.

Directly related to the Bourbon-labor split in the Democratic party was an incident which occurred during the early thirties and which had an important effect on subsequent political developments in the state. Senator Matthew Neely in 1934 supported a rising young "liberal" by the name of Rush Holt for nomination and election as United States Senator from West Virginia. Upon finding himself safely ensconced in that club for six long years, young Rush Holt proved regrettably ungrateful for the favors bestowed upon him by his kindly mentor by deserting the "liberals" for the ranks of the Bourbons. In fact, he forthwith inaugurated a campaign, the purpose of which was the political destruction of Matt Neely.

This incident brought home to Matt Neely the fact that he would never know security so long as the state administration was potentially hostile to his candidacy and, as everyone knows, Matt Neely favors security.

The solution was simple. In typically direct fashion Neely undertook to gather unto himself the state administration.

In 1940 he announced to a grateful state his readiness to forsake the ersatz glamour of our nation's capitol in order to assume the infinitely more important and awful responsibilities of governor of the state. In the primary campaign that followed he succeeded in enlisting the unqualified support of the U.M.W. Matt Neely was not and never has been a "labor candidate." Labor candidates as such have never enjoyed any visible success in West Virginia politics because of the unqualified opposition they earn from other groups in the population. Rather, Matt Neely is all things to all men. He quotes the Bible with passion and eloquence. He inveighs against privilege of every description. And he enjoys and has earned the support of the U.M.W., certain gambling groups, certain coal operators, certain Republican leaders, and many farm leaders. Therefore, even though he and his candidates generally lose most of the conservative sections of the state in Democratic primaries, the margin of defeat is almost invariably narrow.

Matt Neely easily won the 1940 Democratic gubernatorial primary and general election. In addition to obtaining his own nomination and election in 1940, he also succeeded in defeating Rush Holt in the primary and elevated an obscure judge by the name of Kilgore to the office of United States Senator. The Neely group ruled the Democratic party and the state from that November in 1940 until November of 1956, in coalition with the United Mine Workers or "labor" faction of the party.

Two incidents occurred after 1940 which are important in terms of providing insight into the nature of internal Democratic politics. The first was in 1942, when Neely concluded that all the state's problems had been resolved and decided to return to Washington. His fellow citizens, however, denied him this wish in the general election.

The defection from Neely's standard in 1942 was a widespread phenomenon. However, the most important apparent reason for his defeat was the lack of interest displayed by the miners in his candidacy. Neely expected the eastern Bourbon counties to attempt to punish him for snatching the bright Charleston diadem from their crown. But it must have come as a cruel disappointment to him that the miners, too, were so ungrateful as to vote for his opponent in large numbers. Coal strongholds such as Fayette, Raleigh and McDowell counties registered Democratic percentage-point declines of ten or more from 1940-1942.

Bill Blizzard, President, District 17 of the U.M.W., explains the 1942 senatorial election in the following terms: "Old Matt was getting a leetle bit big for his britches. During the entire campaign he didn't come to us once for help or advice. Therefore, we just went fishing on election day. We didn't oppose him, but we didn't work too hard for him either." Blizzard's point was that the coal counties are the domain of the U.M.W., and not the Statehouse. Blizzard's object in the 1942 election was to impress that fact upon Matt Neely.

The second incident was the 1952 Democratic gubernatorial primary, when the Democracy's intraparty

strife was telescoped into one classic battle. In the
Democratic primary of that year the U.M.W. supported a candidate, Hedrick, in opposition to Marland,
the Statehouse candidate. A third candidate by the
name of Homer Kump (son of the former conservative Democratic governor) wore the Bourbon colors.
Therefore, in the 1952 gubernatorial primary the three
principal factions of the Democratic party clashed; the
Bourbons or conservatives, the U.M.W., and the Statehouse group.

An outside observer would have thought the Statehouse group doomed to inevitable defeat. It had lost
its most important block of votes when the miners
defected from the ruling coalition and apparently could
not expect any appreciable conservative support.

Nevertheless, the Neely-Hanna or Statehouse faction
emerged triumphant. The Statehouse group's victory
in the 1952 Democratic primary resulted from three
factors: 1) the strong organizational support which
it received in Republican counties (see Figure 14 for
Republican counties), and in the northern panhandle;
2) the inability of the U.M.W. to carry the coal counties overwhelmingly for its candidate; and 3) the surprising support Marland, the Statehouse candidate,
enjoyed in the conservative eastern counties.

The nature of the Statehouse group's organization
support has been exhaustively examined in preceding
pages. Of more interest was the surprisingly large
vote accorded Marland in the coal and Bourbon counties in the 1952 primary. The reasons for Marland's
success in the coal counties are two-fold. First, many
of the U.M.W. people at the local level have also be-

come Statehouse people. Therefore, in a primary in which the U.M.W. opposed the Statehouse group the local leaders suffered from conflicting loyalties. In 1952, many coal county leaders resolved their dilemma by doing nothing. Secondly, the mine vote is deliverable only when it is in general agreement with its leadership. In addition, the residents of coal communities who are not miners, although often sympathetic with the economic objectives of the union, are notably antipathetic to the idea of union control of the Statehouse.

Marland, the Statehouse candidate, obtained a large vote in the Bourbon counties as a result of a number of factors. In the first place, Governor Patteson, 1948-1952, had done a number of things which pleased the party's Bourbons. Patteson's veto of a "fire boss" bill precipitated U.M.W. opposition to the Statehouse group, as the union regarded passage of the bill as "must" legislation. Therefore, on the theory that if he's "agin him" I'm "fer him," the Statehouse group received support from conservative Democrats. Secondly, Homer Hanna enjoys close personal ties with conservative leaders. Through conferences between Hanna and rural Democrats a number of agreements were reached concerning such matters as the construction and maintenance of parks and the appointment of liquor agents.[1] Thereby, many Bourbon Democratic leaders from rural areas found that they had a vested interest in a Statehouse victory. As a result of all these factors, the Statehouse group was victorious in 1952 in defiance of the laws of political gravity. It

---

[1] Governor Marland is of the opinion that agreements as to parks, patronage and contracts are crucial determinants of victory or defeat in party primaries.

had naught but organizational support and this was sufficient. Thus in the 1952 primary the U.M.W. was also taught that it does not own the state's Democratic organization.

Unlike the other Border States, the Republican party in West Virginia has tasted the sweets of power over a considerable period of the state's history. From 1863 to 1871 and from 1896 to 1932 the Republican party exercised virtually complete control over the state. During the intervening periods the Democratic party has enjoyed control no less complete. Republican partisans hope that their victory in 1956 marks the beginning of yet another extended period of Republican rule.

Like the Democratic party before 1940, the Republican party in West Virginia has always been conservative in character, or "standpat" to use its own terminology. The West Virginia Republicans, like Republicans in other border states, are of two breeds; first, the poor mountain folk who have been Republican since the Civil War, and, secondly, the well-to-do city dwellers who have been Republican since at least 1896.

The poor mountain folk are Republican because they are patriotic and don't believe in rebellions, and because they are conservative. Their conservatism stems from a distrust of change which is characteristic of the isolated person. Change means trouble to these people. From their point of view, a new person or a new idea makes its appearance with but one object in mind, to "fleece" them.

Before 1928 and Walter Hallanan's seizure of Republican power, it was the mountain Republican counties in combination with the traditionally Democratic counties that dominated Republican primaries. In fact, the coalition which nominated Republican candidates was surprisingly similar in character to that which supported successful Democratic candidates for that party's nomination during the same period. The center of gravity of the party rested in the so-called "hardhead" Ohio River Republican counties, counties which have been Republican since the Civil War. These counties are largely rural and rank among the more impoverished in the state. The coal counties, seemingly, were rarely able to unite behind a single Republican primary candiate. There was seldom any important economic reason for the operators to become excited over a Republican primary before 1932. Therefore they largely left politics to the politicians, in the spirit of Kentucky's president of the Louisville and Nashville Railroad Company.

Walter Hallanan's entrance upon the Republican stage in 1928 changed the Republican center of gravity in the same sense and in the same direction as did the Neely-Hanna revolution in the Democratic party. It is West Virginia's coal counties which have furnished Hallanan with his most consistent primary support. However, this does not mean that Hallanan is unpopular in the "hardhead" rural Republican districts. As a matter of fact, he is almost universally respected and liked in these counties. The most convincing evidence of Hallanan's strength in West Virginia's traditionally Republican counties came in the hard-fought 1952 vote for delegates-at-large to the Republican National Convention, when he and his candidates swept the traditionally Republican counties over the Eisenhower candidates. Hallanan's popularity in the traditionally Republican counties is a product of his reputation as the man who held the party together during the "lean" Roosevelt years. However, he does not exercise strong control in the mountain counties because the local organizations have local sources of patronage and funds.

Outside West Virginia, Walter Hallanan is regarded as a conservative Republican. Therefore, it might be concluded that the coal region support received by Hallanan is of an entirely different character from that cast for the Neely-Hanna primary candidates. In truth, the core of Hallanan's support in the coal counties issues from the operators and from local Republican leaders who have no alternative because in these Democratic counties they must rely upon Hallanan for patronage and campaign funds. However, as has already been indicated, Hallanan also relies upon the good graces of Bill Blizzard, District 17, U.M.W. President, for continued control of the coal county Republican organizations. Therefore, Hallanan often turns a sympathetic ear to Blizzard's suggestions relative to candidates and politics.

Bill Blizzard testifies that Hallanan is a "liberal." In his opinion, Hallanan is adverse to the nomination and election of "reactionary" Republican candidates. Hallanan's Republican enemies, such as Millsop, president of Weirton Steel, are also of this opinion. However, they do not attribute these sympathies to any ideological bent. Instead, they point to 1) Hallanan's dependence on the coal counties for control of the Republican party; and 2) the fact that the pre-

1956 absence of Republican senators or representatives from West Virginia in our national capitol gave Hallanan unchallenged control over national patronage.

In a broadside entitled, "What Will You Have, a Hallanan Slate in the Primary or Republican Victory in November? You Cannot Have Both," the Millsop forces said the following about Walter Hallanan in 1952:

> In 1942 Walter Hallanan, although having supported Mr. Revercomb in the Primary elections, failed to do a single thing in the interest of electing Mr. Revercomb. It is reported that he was instrumental in preventing any National Republican funds being made available to assure Mr. Revercomb's election.
>
> It is quite apparent that Mr. Hallanan was not interested in defeating Governor Neely for United States Senator as from the inception of Mr. Neely assuming the office of Governor, the record very definitely discloses Mr. Hallanan as leader of the Republican Party was quite conspicuous by not putting forth any effort whatsoever to defeat Neelyism and this was confirmed by Mr. Hallanan's failure to take any part whatsoever in defeating Mr. Neely for the United States Senate in 1942.
>
> Over this disgraceful period, the fratricidal political dagger of Hallanan was thrust in the backs of Lewis H. Miller, Summers Sharp, Frank Nesbitt, Mont White, and others, in the primaries, in the doublecross that has almost succeeded in bleeding the Republican Party in West Virginia white.

In order to understand why Hallanan might prefer Republican defeat in certain general elections, it is necessary to understand the power structure. As a practical matter, it is more important to Hallanan to defeat his Republican enemies than to elect his Republican friends. If a Democrat is elected Hallanan retains his partonage power within Republican ranks. But if an unfriendly Republican is elected his power suffers diminution. Therefore, Hallanan often has a vested interest in Republican defeat at the polls.

Conclusions

The Statehouse faction of the Democratic party was a tightly knit, well-organized political machine. Its power was based upon the support it customarily received from "organization" counties and from the coal counties. The United Mine Workers union supported Neely-Hanna candidates in most primaries and general elections. However, it was allied with and not a part of the organization group. The United Mine Workers sought to use the coal vote as an instrument for negotiation with the political leaders, in the tradition of pressure groups. The union produced votes for the organization faction, and in return demanded legislative and administrative acts calculated to benefit the union and the men it represents.

The Bourbon Democrats provided a cohesive factional opposition to the labor and Statehouse groups. The Bourbons stand ready when the opportunity presents itself to reassume control of the party. The Bourbons or rural Democrats enjoy much support from industrial and business leaders. In fact, the gentleman farmer of Greenbrier county is often the business leader of Kanawha county.

Therefore, Democratic factionalism is three-sided. In the Democratic party there are: 1) the Bourbons;

2) the United Mine Workers; and 3) the organization group, which continues to exist even though defeated in 1956. The organization, although loosely allied with the U.M.W., acts as a bridge between the Bourbons and the "labor" element in the party. The Bourbons are not ignored by the organization, and the U.M.W. is often disappointed in its demands.

The Republican party was less tightly organized than the Democratic party prior to 1956. Walter Hallanan, the Republican leader, obtained the nomination of his candidates for office for three reasons: 1) control of the Republican organization in the coal and Kanawha Valley counties; 2) close ties with business and union leaders; and 3) the respect accorded him by Republican leaders throughout the state as the man who held the party together during its "lean" years.

No state-wide organizational opposition existed to Hallanan's ascendancy in the Republican party. Several individuals, such as Thomas Millsop of Weirton Steel, disliked him and took advantage of every opportunity to injure him. But no person had appeared with the ability to weld together an effective anti-Hallanan coalition. However, with the ascension of the Republican party to control of the Statehouse and the election of a Republican United States Senator, Hallanan will lose his control over patronage and there will be an inevitable diminution of his political control over the state's Republican party.

The Republican party's economic factions are much less troublesome to its leaders than those of the Democratic party. Few important differences of opinion regarding social and economic policy divide the impoverished Republican farmers and the wealthy urban business leaders.

West Virginia's factionalism demonstrates one of the more interesting and distinctive features of the Border State political scene. Until relatively recently, West Virginia's Northern stock was Republican and the Southern stock Democratic. Since the New Deal certain labor groups and a good many Negroes have entered the Democratic party. Therefore, the comfortable Civil War dichotomy between the parties is becoming blurred with the passage of time.

CHAPTER V

WEST VIRGINIA TRENDS

THE COMPOSITION of a political party is a major determinant of its factionalism and political organization. Political change alters the composition of parties. And a change in the composition of a political party inevitably results in a new kind of factionalism and political organization. Therefore, an understanding of the nature of political change is basic to a study of political parties. Our attention is now centered on political change in West Virginia; how, why, and where it has occurred.

The Background

West Virginians believe in the right of a man to change his mind, but they are not frivolous in the exercise of this right. From 1872 to 1956, the Democratic party was victorious in the state in twelve presidential elections and the Republicans in ten.

In view of this record, the casual observer might be pardoned for thinking of West Virginia in terms of a political danseuse, skipping with gay abandon from party to party. Such is not the case. Eight of the ten Republican victories occurred in the elections from 1896 through 1928. The voters have been similarly constant in their relations with the Democratic party. Democratic victories have taken place from 1876 through 1892, 1932 through 1952, and 1912.

Figure 14 identifies the Democratic and Republican counties of the state. There are two categories of

Democratic counties in terms of the point in time at which they became Democratic. Sixteen counties have been Democratic almost without exception in presidential elections since Civil War days. Eleven of the sixteen consistently Democratic counties are among the state's twenty-seven most rural counties (those one-third rural farm or more in 1950). Four of the eleven rural Democratic counties (Jefferson, Hampshire, Hardy and Greenbrier), ranging along the southern border of the state, are among the seven West Virginia counties which had 1,000 or more slaves in 1860. The rural West Virginia Democrats are variously referred to in the state as conservatives, rural Democrats, "Old Dominion" Democrats, and Bourbons. The traditionally Democratic counties were settled at an early period and primarily by Southerners. Boone, Logan and Mingo, alone, of the sixteen long-time Democratic counties, are coal counties. All three counties were conservative strongholds of the Democratic party before 1932. However, the Democratic leadership in these counties was captured by U.M.W.-oriented Democrats after 1932, and the counties now cast pluralities in favor of "liberal" candidates in Democratic primaries.

The second category of Democratic counties consists of those which joined the party as a result of the New Deal period. There are twelve such counties of which ten are important coal producing areas and two are metropolitan areas. Hancock and Brooke, the two metropolitan areas in the group, are steel-producing communities.

The traditionally (or "Ohio River Hardhead") Republican counties are located along the Ohio River

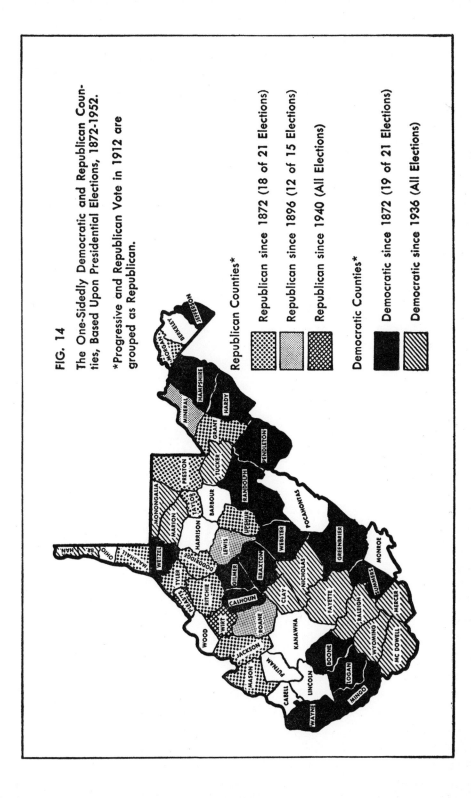

FIG. 14

The One-Sidedly Democratic and Republican Counties, Based Upon Presidential Elections, 1872-1952.

*Progressive and Republican Vote in 1912 are grouped as Republican.

Republican Counties*

Republican since 1872 (18 of 21 Elections)

Republican since 1896 (12 of 15 Elections)

Republican since 1940 (All Elections)

Democratic Counties*

Democratic since 1872 (19 of 21 Elections)

Democratic since 1936 (All Elections)

from Mason county on the south to Marshall on the
north and along the northern border of the state from
Morgan county on the east to Preston on the west.
Eight of the eleven traditionally Republican counties
are among the twenty-seven most rural counties in
the state. Eight are also among the twenty-six poorest
West Virginia counties (in which more than 48 per
cent of the families had incomes of $2000 per year
or less in 1950). Two West Virginia counties are
recent converts to the Republican faith. The two
counties which have shifted from the Democratic
party to Republican ranks since 1940 are rural farm,
low-income communities.

The majority of both the traditionally Democratic
and Republican counties are rural. The traditionally
Democratic counties are largely in the southern portion of the state. Many of them were important slave
centers prior to the Civil War and were largely settled
by Southerners. The Republican counties are in the
northern portion of the state. There were few slave-
holdings in these counties, and the early settlers
tended to be from Northern communities. The counties which have become Democratic since 1932 are
entirely different in social and economic terms from
those which have been traditionally Democratic. These
newcomers to the Democratic hosts are mining and
steel centers with a large laboring population, and the
vote cast by their citizenry is a lower socio-economic
"class vote."

Recent Political Change

Political change in West Virginia since 1916, as reflected in Figure 15, occurred, principally, in three

areas of the state: 1) the coal counties, 2) the isolated, low-income rural counties, and 3) the traditionally Democratic or Bourbon counties. The absence of the colored factor in West Virginia's political change equation represents a fourth topic of discussion in this section.

1. *The Coal Counties*

It would be repetitious to deal at length with the reasons for the considerable plus Democratic trend of the West Virginia coal counties. This topic has been treated in detail in the chapter dealing with Kentucky trends. Suffice it to say, that of the eleven West Virginia counties which registered a 15 percentage-point increase or more in Democratic vote over the period 1916-1952, nine are among the ten most important coal producing counties in the state (see Figure 16). The tenth coal county, Kanawha county, is a special case which is examined later in this section.

Of interest, relative to the change in the mine vote, are the reasons given by a West Virginia mine foreman for the tendency of coal miners to vote as a block. According to the foreman, the dangerous life the men lead teaches them that group effort is essential for survival. Then, too, such a life develops a feeling of comradeship absent in more sedate professions, a proposition to which most old infantrymen will subscribe. Secondly, according to the foreman, life in a mining camp tends to promote group behavior. Most urban folk have neighbors who follow many different professions and who have many different points of view. In a mining camp, coal dominates the minds and actions of virtually everyone. This environment

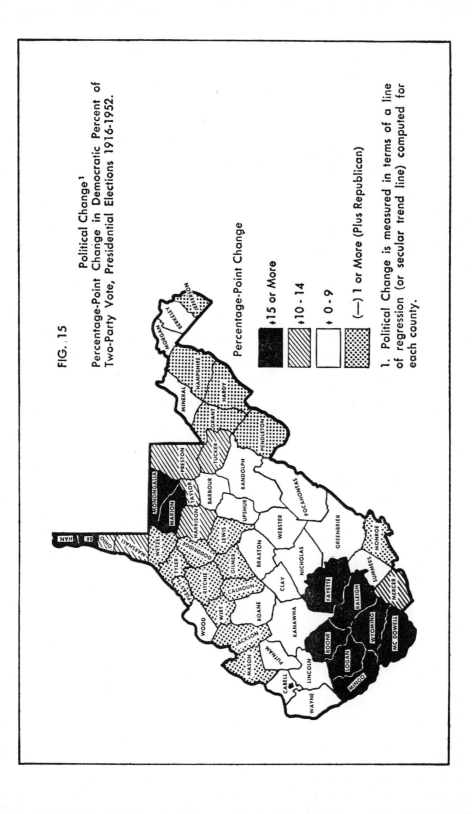

FIG. 15

Political Change[1]

Percentage-Point Change in Democratic Percent of
Two-Party Vote, Presidential Elections 1916-1952.

Percentage-Point Change

↕15 or More

↕10 - 14

↕ 0 - 9

(—) 1 or More (Plus Republican)

1. Political Change is measured in terms of a line
of regression (or secular trend line) computed for
each county.

produces an outlook and a type of political behavior qualitatively and quantitatively different from that of the average community.

In an effort to illustrate the type of behavior pattern produced by the coal mine environment, the foreman tells a story, possibly apocryphal, of a strike. A miner, it seems, approached a water bucket less out of thirst than for diversion. He lifted the cup to his lips, sipped, then dashed the contents to the ground in a spirit of absent-minded vigor. His companions, observing his actions, assumed that something was wrong with the water. They thereupon dropped their tools and went on strike. The miner who spilled the water, assuming something had occurred that had escaped his eye, wordlessly followed his companions' example. A strike was on.

The purpose of the story was to make more vivid by exaggeration the character or culture traits which made possible the mass desertion of one political party in favor of another on the part of the miners. The miners were hungry. The New Deal offered them succor, and their leaders recommended that they respond with their votes. Almost to a man, they dropped their Republican voting habits and voted Democratic.

However, if so many miners switched to the Democratic party after 1932, why did Kanawha county, which contains the fifth largest mining population in the state (1950 census), register only a modest increase in its percentage Democratic vote? Kanawha county is located in West Virginia's wealthy "Magic Valley," formed by the Kanawha River. Charleston, the capital of the state, is located in the county. The population of the county was 239,000 in 1950, making it the most populous county of the state. The county, in addition to being a mining center, is the locale of a large and growing chemical industry. In 1950, approximately 9000 of the county's workers were employed as coal miners, and 21,000 in manufacturing establishments, whereas only 1000 people were classified as agricultural employees.

Politically, the county was narrowly divided between the two major parties prior to 1896, was largely Republican between 1896 and 1932, and since 1932 has cast initially large but steadily diminishing Democratic majorities. In 1952, the county returned to the Republican fold.

Kanawha county deserves special attention because conditions there reflect changes that are occurring throughout the state. Industrial development is expanding at a rapid rate, whereas mining activity has tended to stabilize or contract. An important question for West Virginia politicians, therefore, is the political potential of this secular change in the social and economic character of the county and state.

The answer seems to be that in large measure the change is operating to the advantage of the Republican party. West Virginia's Attorney General Fox gives two reasons for this phenomenon: 1) the chemical industry is expanding and pays relatively high wages; 2) the industry tends to employ a high proportion of professional people, or people who like to think of themselves as "professional" rather than as workers. These people range all the way from the minor technicians to senior scientists. Thus both the wages paid

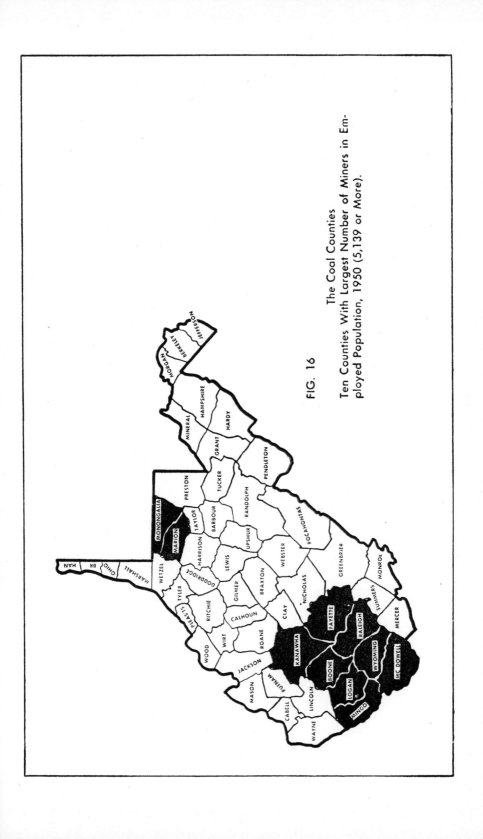

FIG. 16

The Coal Counties

Ten Counties With Largest Number of Miners in Employed Population, 1950 (5,139 or More).

and the nature of the work militate against the development of a "labor" psychology. The tendency then is for the chemical industry workers to identify themselves with management. The result is an increasing Republican vote.

It is thought by many West Virginia politicians that if present trends continue that the state will once again join the ranks of the Republican party. These trends are: 1) a reduction in the number of people employed in the coal mines, a trend which means a reduced Democratic vote; 2) the growth of the chemical industry which seemingly means an increase in the state's Republican vote; and 3) the tendency of rural areas to vote more Republican.

2. The Low Income Rural Counties

The isolated, impoverished rural areas of West Virginia have behaved quite differently politically than the coal counties. Comparison of Figure 17, showing the state's low income counties, with Figure 15, identifying the locale and nature of political change, reveals that fifteen of the seventeen counties which have experienced a plus Republican change since 1916 are also among the least wealthy counties of the state.

Dr. Smith, a former Republican county chairman in Gilmer county, advances one plausible reason for the political behavior of the state's low income counties. Dr. Smith observed, "We have no organized groups here, such as unions"; meaning, few countervailing organized groups exist in such low income counties outside the business and political communities. Assuming that Dr. Smith's analysis is accurate, the question still remains whether lack of organization as such is the cause of plus Republican change, or whether it is due to the resentment of the organized business groups in the low income counties to the activities of other organized groups in the state.

A partial answer to the question is to be found in the fact that the poor farmer and the unorganized workman probably benefited least from New Deal measures in an economic sense. Therefore, these people tend to resent the widely publicized gains enjoyed by such groups as the miners. They compare invidiously their economic status with the wages of union workers. The comparison, interestingly enough, stimulates resentment against the union rather than against the people who pay their wages.

However, more important than the attitudes of individual farmers and workers is the fact that organized labor has wrested political control of the state from the low income Republican counties as well as from the rural Democratic counties. As the discussion in Chapter IV indicated, the rural or Bourbon Democrats ruled the Democratic party prior to 1940 and the rural Republicans were dominant in the Republican party before 1928. The center of power for both parties has shifted to the coal counties, which are also the centers of organized labor's power in the state. The leaders in the low-income counties blame the New Deal for labor's power. Therefore, they hold the Democratic party responsible for the diminution in power that they have suffered.

Table 6 demonstrates the relationship which exists in the state between the economic level of the counties and their tendency to cast fewer Democratic

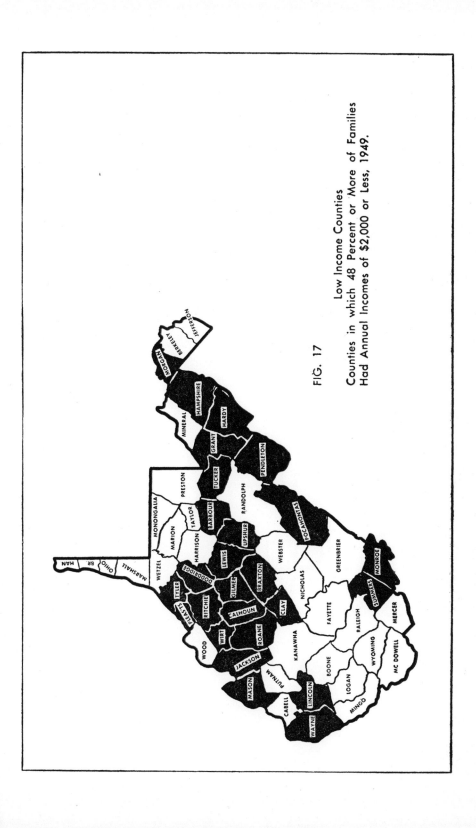

FIG. 17

Low Income Counties
Counties in which 48 Percent or More of Families
Had Annual Incomes of $2,000 or Less, 1949.

TABLE 6

RELATIONSHIP BETWEEN INCOME LEVEL AND POLITICAL
CHANGE — WEST VIRGINIA

% Families with Income less than $2,000, 1949	No. of Counties	Mean % Point Change in Democratic Vote, 1916-1952
60%	11	—4.0
50-59%	12	1.0
40-49%	13	4.6
30-39%	7	15.8
20-29%	10	16.8
10-19%	2	33.7
Totals	55	6.6

votes, proportionately; i.e., the poorer the county the more likely it is to show an increasing tendency to vote Republican in presidential elections. Reference to Table 6 shows that the very poorest counties in West Virginia (those in which 60 per cent or more receive income less than $2,000) are the only group to show a mean percentage-point decline in Democratic vote, 1916-1952. The most wealthy counties on the other hand have registered a mean increase in Democratic vote of 34 percentage-points.

Table 7 separates from Table 6 the counties in which 50 per cent or more of the population was rural farm, in 1950. The purpose of Table 7 is to determine whether the same relationship between income level and tendency to vote Democratic exists among the rural counties as Table 6 showed exists among all the counties of the state.

As Table 7 indicates, an identical relationship exists. However, as the Table also shows, a relationship exists between rural farm and income level and rural farm and political change. Thus because rural farm status

TABLE 7
WEST VIRGINIA COUNTIES 50% OR MORE RURAL FARM—
RELATIONSHIP BETWEEN ECONOMIC LEVEL
AND POLITICAL CHANGE

% of Families with Incomes less than $2,000, 1949	No. of Counties	Mean % Point Democratic Change, 1916-1952	Mean % Rural Farm 1950
65 or More	6	—3.5	62
60-64%	4	—2.5	60
55-59%	3	—1.8	55
50-54%	1	+8.1	53

and poverty are synonymous in West Virginia it is difficult to establish which, if either, might be the determinant of plus Republican change. However, when the political behavior of the low-income West Virginia counties is compared with that of the rural counties of Missouri, Kentucky, and Maryland, a pattern develops. In all the Border States the low-income rural counties tend to register a plus Republican trend. However, many of the more well-to-do rural farm counties of Kentucky and Missouri (such as the Pennyroyal section of Kentucky and Missouri's Cotton Delta) have tended to vote increasingly Democratic since 1916, primarily because of the economic benefits derived from the New Deal farm program in these counties. Consequently, the low-income factor would seem to be the most important variable explaining plus Republican change. But, where the Bourbon elements have felt threatened by the New Deal, plus Republican change has also occurred in more wealthy rural areas.

3. *The Bourbon Counties*

Four of the seven West Virginia counties which had a slave population of more than 1,000 in 1860 are counted among the seventeen counties which have experienced a decline in their percentage Democratic vote. The reasons for the tendency of West Virginia's Bourbon counties to cast a larger Republican vote, proportionately, are similar to those cited for the low income counties, i.e., loss of party control to the United Mine Workers and the faction which presently controls the Statehouse. The Bourbons no longer have a strong incentive to work for the election of a Democratic ticket. Not all Bourbon leaders, by any means, have defected from the Democratic party, but the intensity of their interest in the results of elections has diminished.

The assignment of reasons for the defection of West Virginia's Bourbon counties is further clouded by the fact that except for fertile valleys the greater part of most of the Bourbon counties are as impoverished as other rural areas of the state. Therefore, some of the plus Republican trend in the so-called Bourbon counties might be accounted for by the same factors responsible for the plus Republican trend in the northern low-income counties. Jefferson county, however, in the Shenandoah Valley, is a relatively prosperous Bourbon-type community, and it has registered a decline in its percentage Democratic vote.

4. *The West Virginia Negro*

In 1900 the colored population of West Virginia was 5 per cent of the total population, whereas in 1950 it represented 6 per cent of the population. Though the proportion that the West Virginia Negro represents of the total population has changed very little, his physical location has undergone the most radical kind of change. Since 1900, the tendency has been for the coal and urban communities to attract Negroes, whereas the old plantation sections have lost much of their Negro population. The type of population shift is not surprising, but its degree is astonishing. Many of the old Bourbon counties are almost without a colored population, whereas the coal counties have become the home of more than 50 per cent of the state's Negroes.

"Cap" Ferguson is a colored political figure who makes his home in Charleston. Mr. Ferguson is a Republican and classifies himself as a Hallanan supporter. He is one of the more important of the state's Negro politicians. Ferguson, however, is more than a Republican and a political figure. He is a man who works tirelessly to better the position of his race. The following is essentially Ferguson's interpretation of the role of the Negro in West Virginia politics.

The Negro was imported into West Virginia *en masse* by the coal operators. They had two reasons for bringing the Negro into the state to work in the mines: 1) he represented a source of cheap and abundant labor; and 2) he was amenable to discipline. As a by-product of both these factors, the Negro became an important block vote which was manipulable by the operators almost at will.

Ferguson was a political leader during a portion of this period. Was he extremely unhappy about this situation? Did he rebel against operator domination? The answer is "No," and for some very good reasons. In the first place, because the Negro was easily handled and would not join unions or go on strike, he was often placed in positions of authority and responsibility. Consequently, the relative position of the Negro in the coal industry was probably as good as that of any industry in the country. The Negro knew that he could not expect similar treatment at the hands of his white fellow workers. He therefore voted his own self-interest when he voted as the mine owner dictated.

U.M.W. leaders soon found that it was necessary to enlist the colored man alongside the white if they were to organize the industry. The union also found that it was impossible to enlist them as second-class union citizens because of their numbers and power. Therefore, the Negro has achieved a status in the U.M.W. on a par with other union members. In this case an apparent evil has produced a social revolution which many would regard as "good."

The effect that union membership has had upon Negro political behavior has been pronounced. Before 1932 and unionization, the Negro voted as a member of the colored group, usually casting his ballot as the state-wide Negro leader wished. Today the Negro in the coal counties does not vote as a colored man but as a miner. His vote is solicited and obtained by his union leader rather than by the state-wide Negro leader.

"Cap" Ferguson regrets this development. According to him, it has reduced the voice of the Negro in state politics to a mute whisper. However, in terms of the long-run integration of the Negro into the greater society, this development has implications which may be more important than an FEPC law.

Conclusions

The political change that has occurred in West Virginia is, to a considerable extent, responsible for the form of factionalism that exists within the state's political parties. In turn, the factionalism with which the Democratic party is plagued is an important cause of the state's political change.

The Neely-Hanna forces, in alliance with the U.M.W., captured the Democratic party of the state in 1940. It was the New Deal and the enlistment of the coal miners in Democratic ranks that made possible this revolution in the structure of the state's Democratic party. The Bourbons now find themselves in a subordinate position within a party which they regard as dominated by labor elements. Therefore, they have shown a tendency to defect from the Democratic party.

All counties which were strongly Republican after the Civil War and have remained largely rural farm have maintained their alliance with the Republican party, and in most cases have become increasingly Republican since 1916. The principal reasons for the plus Republican trend of these counties are: 1) the feeling on the part of many of the citizenry that they did not enjoy an equal share in the economic gains of the New Deal period; 2) resentment against labor groups, and particularly the U.M.W. which has exercised a commanding voice in state politics in recent years; 3) the absence of any organized force in the rural Republican communities to counterbalance the influence and power of such people and groups as bankers, Chambers of Commerce, lawyers and doctors.

The coal counties and the northern panhandle urban communities have experienced a pronounced plus Democratic trend for reasons just the reverse of those for the plus Republican trend in the rural counties. The New Deal ushered in an era of unprecedented power for organized labor in West Virginia. The suggestions of union presidents carry at least as much weight with the political authorities as those of corporation presidents. The increased power of organized labor has been translated into higher wages and better working conditions for the laborers. The New Deal and the Democratic party have been identified with these advances in the position of organized labor. The result has been a tremendous outpouring of Democratic votes, most of which have remained Democratic, even in the face of the Eisenhower personality.

Political change, in a sense, is the gyroscope of the two-party system. Shifts in the relative strength and composition of political parties reveal much concerning the nature of the two-party system, and the process by which parties stay in balance.

CHAPTER VI

SECTIONALISM AND FACTIONALISM IN MISSOURI

LINCOLN STEFFENS, the great muckraker, visited St. Louis at the turn of the century and came away shuddering at the murky quality of both its drinking water and its politics. Forty years later like-minded visitors remained glued to their railway chairs at the St. Louis stop, their destination being Tom Pendergast's Kansas City. In the Kansas City of 1940, the latter-day muckraker found the water clear and clean, but the politics at least as turgid as in St. Louis in 1900.

The political history of Missouri since 1900 has been, to a very considerable extent, the history of the rise and decline of both machines and reform movements in its two great cities.

Political Organization in Missouri

The basic structure of Missouri's political spectrum is similar to that of the other Border States. The Little Dixie section in northeastern Missouri was originally settled by slave-owners, and represents a continuing source of Bourbon Democratic strength. The southwestern Ozark section was settled by hill people from Tennessee and Kentucky and has been a strongly Republican section since the Civil War.[1] However, the Bourbons have never been strong enough numerically to dominate the state's Democratic party. But though they have rarely, if ever, exercised con-

---

[1] See Chapter I for a detailed discussion of the settlement pattern in Missouri.

trolling power in the state, neither have they been out of power. Through alliances with urban politicians and special interest groups, and through the investment of their intellectual and monetary capital they have maintained a prominent position in the councils of the Democratic party.

The locus of "organization" strength in Missouri is also similar to the pattern in the other Border States. Ten of the 31 Missouri counties which habitually support the Democratic "organization" candidate[1] are located in the Republican southwestern Ozarks, and seven are traditionally Democratic or Bourbon counties. The important points underlined by the pattern of organization strength in Missouri are: 1) many of the Republican mountain counties of Missouri, as in West Virginia and Kentucky, are "organization" counties which are almost invariably carried by the dominant group in the Democratic party; 2) the state's Bourbons have almost invariably been represented in the Democratic party's dominant group.

Within this Border State environment, the big city politicians have occupied a central place on the political stage. Ed Butler was the St. Louis political boss in 1900. He was a Democrat in a Republican town and was "the boss." The Republican administrations in St. Louis did not have any control over appointments to the city's police department and election boards because a "reform-minded" Democratic governor and legislature had deprived the city of the power to appoint these officials, their laudable motive being the eradication of political corruption (Repub-

---

[1] Counties which cast plurality for victorious candidate in 10 or more Democratic gubernatorial primaries, 1908-1952.

lican, that is) in that notoriously wicked city. Not
unnaturally, the Democratic governor placed great re-
liance on Butler's recommendations relative to appointments to the St. Louis police department and election
board, and this, of course, was the source of Mr.
Butler's power in the city. In return, Butler was always amenable to suggestions of party leaders relative
to the vote of the St. Louis delegation at conventions
and in the legislature.

However, Ed Butler made a mistake. On one otherwise lovely day, he persuaded a Mr. Joseph Folk to
run for circuit attorney of the city. Folk was elected,
and, lamentably, proved to be a man without honor.
He investigated charges of corruption with distressing
vigor. He soon discovered that the city's legislators
had gone so far as to draw up schedules of bribes
for various grants and other favors.[1] These grants
included such items as railway franchises, streets,
street lights, and rights-of-way for side tracks. Most
distressing of all, though, Folk then proceeded to
prosecute the bribers as well as the bribed. Million-
aires and wardheelers were called into court. Finally,
in a crowning gesture of ingratitude, Folk brought his
benefactor, Ed Butler, to trial.

Joe Folk rode his reform horse to the office of governor. However, the effect on Missouri's Democratic
party was little short of disastrous. St. Louis was left
without a Democratic organization. In addition, the
Democratic party had been identified with corruption
in the minds of many rural Missourians. As a result,
for two decades the great political question in Missouri was to be the size of the Republican vote in the

---

[1] Lincoln Steffens, *The Shame of the Cities* (New York, 1948), p. 33.

St. Louis area. In most elections from 1904 and until 1932, it was large enough to elect a Republican governor and carry the state for Republican candidates for president.

The political demise of Tom Pendergast in 1940 was an event very nearly as disastrous to Democratic fortunes in the state as was Ed Butler's disillusioning experience at the turn of the century.[1] Tom Pendergast came to Kansas City in 1890 at the age of 18. He joined his brother, Jim, who had already attained recognition as a political leader. The two brothers operated a saloon and worked on the formation of a political organization. Jim taught his brother, Tom, that the science of politics consisted of such things as doorbell ringing, giving out free food and coal, helping the local clergy, and acting as a mediator with the police.[2]

Tom Pendergast did not become absolute boss of Kansas City until 1930. In the interim Pendergast fought for control of the city's Democratic party with the so-called Shannon faction. Finally, Pendergast and Shannon wearied of the factional strife and a truce was arranged whereby patronage was divided on a 50-50 basis. In 1930, Shannon was elected to the United States House of Representatives, and Pendergast was left in undisputed control of the Democratic machine.

More important than the resolution of factional strife in Pendergast's elevation to the role of Kansas

---

[1] The greater part of this analysis of Kansas City politics is taken from a detailed study made by John Oliver, Attorney, and a leader in the City's reform movement. Mr. Oliver's study has not been published. Any interpretation or opinion expressed is the author's, and not Mr. Oliver's.

[2] Maurice M. Milligan, *Inside Story of the Pendergast Machine*, (New York, 1948), p. 47.

City "boss" was the passage of a new Kansas City charter in 1925. The 1925 Kansas City charter was designed to be a reform document. It provided for the appointment of a city manager and a more "democratic" selection of city councilmen. Tom Pendergast declared himself an unswerving supporter of scientific government and democracy, and exerted himself in behalf of the measure.

Dumbfounded Kansas Citians soon discovered the reasons for Pendergast's unorthodox behavior. As it developed, the democratic features of the charter resulted in the election of more Pendergast-backed councilmen than had been possible under the old charter. According to the reform charter, four of the city's nine councilmen were elected "at large." Therefore, Pendergast was able to put his enormous northwest Kansas City majorities to good use in electing candidates to fill the four at-large seats and thereby gained control of the city council.

In common with most urban political machines, Tom Pendergast's political strength was centered in the less well-to-do sections of the city. Kansas City election returns during the Pendergast period had all the coloration of a rich versus poor struggle. The most consistently Democratic wards during Pendergast's reign were located in the northwestern corner of the city. Ward 1, where Democratic or Pendergast strength was greatest, is sometimes called the "flophouse" ward. South and east of Ward 1 are the wards with large colored and immigrant populations where the Democrats also compiled impressive majorities. According to the 1930 census, the "north end" of Kansas City (the Pendergast preserve), including Wards 1, 2, 3, 4,

9 and 11, had a population of 122,000, of whom 44 per cent were colored, 30 per cent foreign born and 26 per cent native white.[1]

South of the Democratic low income wards are located the more "desirable" residential areas of the city. The 8th ward in the extreme southwest corner of the city is the "silk stocking" district. The 8th ward provided majorities for Republican and "reform" candidates during the Pendergast period almost as consistently as Ward 1 produced pluralities for Democratic or "machine" hopefuls. Appearances to the contrary notwithstanding, however, the Kansas City political alignment was not a simple economic division between the haves and have nots. The paradoxical nature of the Kansas City political alignment can be appreciated only when it is realized that Pendergast enjoyed his power on the sufferance or in many cases because of the active support of the business leaders of the community. The business community supported or tolerated Pendergast out of gratitude for services rendered, such as low assessment rates on property, real estate investment tips, franchises granted, law infractions overlooked. Then why did the silk stocking districts oppose Pendergast? And why did the depressed population support him? And let it be said that while there was a good deal of "counting" and "repeating" in Kansas City's depressed areas, nonetheless the residents of the city's low-income wards cast their votes willingly for the Pendergast candidates.

The answer to the first question is to be found in middle-class ethics. Most solid citizens felt that Tom Pendergast was a "bad" man. Furthermore, if an

---

[1] Oliver, "Study of Kansas City Politics," (unpublished).

"honest" businessman's government were elected they anticipated retaining all the advantages of boss rule with none of the attendant disadvantages. It was impossible to elect a Republican. Therefore, resort was made to the reform expedient.

The reasons for the support given Pendergast by depressed elements of Kansas City's population were detailed by a colored newspaperman as follows: "We knew the Pendergast people at the precinct and ward level. They came to us and asked us what we wanted and needed. When we wanted something done or needed a job or were in trouble we could turn to the Pendergast precinct or ward leader for help. And they produced for us. I have never seen a reform person down here in our sections. They never ask us for favors. We can't ask them for favors."

In other words, the Pendergast organization provided a much needed link between the governed and the governors. The well-to-do rarely find it difficult to bring their wishes to the attention of the rulers. However, the immigrants, the poor, the colored, those engaged in borderline enterprises find it difficult to get their day in court. In return for their votes, the Pendergast organization attempted to satisfy the more pressing day-to-day needs of these people.

The vote is a very effective tool owned by low income groups by which they can attempt to better their social and economic position. The Pendergast machine paid the immigrants, the colored, the dispossessed for the use of this tool. They paid in a variety of tender that was more important than greenbacks to the people of northwest Kansas City. If a bewildered and friendless Negro or immigrant were called into court on some minor charge, his Democratic precinct leader was often able to have the charge dismissed. If a small storekeeper or bookie or vendor were arrested for the violation of some "obscure" ordinance, his Pendergast leader was available to render aid and comfort to the defendant. A free drink for the bums, a job for the unemployed—these were the stock in trade of the Pendergast machine.[1]

On election day the Pendergast precinct leaders demanded payment for services rendered. The majorities cast by the low-income wards for Pendergast-backed candidates testify to the high political credit rating of these people, and to the energy of Pendergast's lieutenants. The first or "Flophouse" Ward, for example, cast pluralities for Pendergast mayoralty candidates which reached astronomical heights during the thirties. The first ward pluralities precipitously declined after 1938 when the Pendergast machine was overtaken by reform.[2]

Thus the Pendergast machine performed a double-edged service for the lower socio-economic groups. In addition to filling their "bellies," it produced one-sided political majorities from the depressed areas, thus maximizing the importance of the low-income vote. Thereby the spokesmen for the low-income groups were in a position to demand special privileges from the political authorities.

In 1936, Tom Pendergast made a mistake. He supported Lloyd C. Stark for governor. In the 1936

---

[1] Milligan, *Pendergast Machine*, p. 47.

[2] The pluralities cast by the first ward for Pendergast-backed mayoralty candidates were as follows:

1930	1934	1938	1940
7,250	17,500	10,000	3,300

Democratic gubernatorial primary, Pendergast delivered a vote from Jackson County of 170,000 for Stark as opposed to only 3,000 votes for his opponent. Mr. Stark proved to be another "dishonest" man. Once nominated and elected he proceeded to "clean-up" Kansas City politics. The clean-up did not end until Tom Pendergast was deposited in the penitentiary and the Kansas City Democratic machine was liquidated.

Since 1940 and the disappearance of Tom Pendergast, the "silk stocking" wards have maximized the importance of their vote and minimized the importance of the low-income vote. Therefore, the Negro, the immigrant, the dispossessed have lost one of their most important tools in their never-ending social and economic struggle. In place of a corrupt machine, a bright and shining government of "honest businessmen" rules. The businessmen no longer need pay for low assessments. They are granted them as a matter of right.

The demise of Tom Pendergast's Kansas City political machine has had many repercussions on Democratic fortunes in the state. In presidential elections the Kansas City percentage Democratic vote has declined from a figure in excess of 60 per cent during the thirties to one approaching the 50 per cent level in more recent elections. The reason for the decline in the vote for national Democratic candidates is the fact that no one gets out the low-income vote as efficiently as did Tom Pendergast. More importantly, perhaps, the unceremonious departure of Tom Pendergast from the state's political stage left the Democratic party rudderless. Unlike West Virginia and Kentucky,

Missouri does not have a tradition of strong executive leadership. In the absence of leadership by the governor, party control has tended to drift into the hands of strong political leaders such as Tom Pendergast or combinations of local political leaders and representatives of powerful interest groups.

The principal reason for the lack of central direction of Missouri's Democratic party is that the state has a "weak" governor. The adjective "weak" as used here does not refer to the character of the occupant of the office. Instead, it refers to his power. In Missouri, many of the tools of power have been removed from the governor's hands and placed in the care of independent boards and commissions. The Highway Department, for example, is almost completely divorced from the governor. The governing body of the Department consists of a non-salaried bi-partisan State Highway Commission, appointed by the governor for staggered six-year terms. The Commission appoints the chief engineer, a professional person (non-political), who is responsible for administering the highway program. Employment with the Highway Department is on a bi-partisan basis and made without reference to the governor's wishes. The Conservation Department has also been divorced from "politics." Control of the Department is in the hands of a bi-partisan Board under terms similar to those of the Highway Department. Within the Conservation Department, but outside even its control, is a State Park Board appointed by the governor for staggered four-year terms.

Because of the limited patronage and related power he enjoys, the Missouri governor has little power over the actions of his legislature. Because of this same disability he has even less authority over the actions of party leaders in the primaries. Finally, the governor is denied the opportunity to seek office for two consecutive terms by a constitutional provision. Therefore, there is little continuity in the programs of Missouri governors. They are each limited to four-year terms and when their short period in office is terminated so is the entire policy orientation which they have attempted to inspire.

Because of the absence of executive leadership and because of his control over a large block of votes, Tom Pendergast was able to dictate the selection of Democratic nominees for state-wide offices during the thirties. Pendergast became the dominant figure in Missouri politics during the thirties because of the awesome pluralities he could register from Kansas City for Democratic primary candidates for state-wide office. For example, in the primaries from 1928 through 1936 the pluralities from Jackson county (Kansas City) cast for the Pendergast-backed gubernatorial candidates were as follows: in 1928, the Jackson county pro-Pendergast plurality was 48,000 votes; in 1932, 100,000 votes; and in 1936, 165,000 votes. Since Pendergast's departure in 1940, the Jackson county vote has been very nearly evenly divided between the two leading candidates for the Democratic gubernatorial nomination.

It was in 1932 that Pendergast became the true "boss" of Missouri's Democratic party. The occasion for his assumption of near-absolute authority was the governor's veto in 1931 of a congressional re-districting act. The governor's veto of the re-districting act made necessary the nomination and election "at large" of all candidates for the United States House of Representatives. Therefore, Pendergast's Kansas City majorities became an important factor in the nomination and election of Missouri's United States Representatives, as well as for the major state offices. Important Democrats from throughout the state descended on Kansas City to pay homage to the king, and, incidentally, to obtain his support in the primary. Support was not granted without a price, and a part of the price was local support of Pendergast-backed candidates for state office.

Table 8 tells the tale of the 1932 Democratic primary. There were fifty-six candidates for Missouri's thirteen seats in the United States House of Representatives. Therefore, the vote of the rural counties was rather generously distributed among favorite son candidates, while the Kansas City vote was conveniently concentrated on just a few of Mr. Pendergast's "ponies." Eight Pendergast-backed candidates received 80 thousand or more votes from Kansas City and were also nominated and elected. Two candidates were nominated, Romjure and Williams, who received less than 20 thousand Kansas City votes but only because of overwhelming outstate support. However, only one strongly backed Pendergast-backed candidate was defeated and all others nominated and elected. Comparison of the votes received in Kansas City by candidates not supported by Pendergast with those received by the Pendergast-backed candidates clearly demonstrates the decisive influence of the Kansas City machine vote in the primary.

Due to his control over the Kansas City vote,

TABLE 8

PENDERGAST RULES THE STATE

Vote for Representatives to Congress in Democratic Primary,
State of Missouri, August 2, 1932, Eighteen Leading
Candidates

	The Pendergast-Backed Candidates				
	Claiborne*	Cockran*	Duncan*	Lee*	Ruffin*
Kansas City	80,175	82,972	80,561	85,000	80,703
State Outside City	102,964	229,244	107,554	95,307	109,749
Total Vote	183,139	312,216	188,115	180,307	190,452
	Shannon*	Taylor	Wood*	Cannon*	Lozier*
Kansas City	97,110	80,799	81,743	61,270	63,917
State Outside City	237,208	87,087	97,923	183,512	175,366
Total Vote	334,318	167,886	179,666	244,782	239,283

	Those Not Backed by Pendergast			
	Barton	Dickmann*	Fulbright	Johnson
Kansas City	5,795	38,511	7,103	4,874
State Outside City	140,383	157,361	159,763	150,180
Total Vote	146,178	195,872	166,866	155,054
	Milligan*	Nelson	Romjure*	Williams*
Kansas City	44,260	12,791	13,560	19,394
State Outside City	154,322	158,519	171,811	184,209
Total Vote	198,582	171,310	185,371,	203,603

* Nominated

Pendergast exerted a decisive influence over the nomination and election of Democratic candidates. Therefore, the successful Democratic candidates tended to
listen with care to Pendergast's suggestions relative to
appointments and administrative acts. As a result, his
influence spread beyond the confines of the Jackson
county area as more and more influential Missourians

incurred political debts to the Kansas City leader. Not unnaturally, the majority of Pendergast's contacts were in the western part of the state, partially because of geographic propinquity and partially because of a common desire to promote the interests of the western part of the state.

Figure 18 demonstrates the value of Pendergast's outstanding political credits in western Missouri. The figure shows that in the Democratic gubernatorial primaries from 1928 through 1936 the overwhelming majority of the counties in the western part of the state and in portions of "Little Dixie" consistently cast a plurality for the Pendergast-backed candidates whereas the eastern counties tended to oppose the Pendergast-backed candidates. Consequently, Pendergast never had to rely solely upon the Jackson county vote for victory for his candidates.

The political death of the Pendergast machine shifted the state's center of political gravity to St. Louis. Mayor Dickmann of St. Louis had been active during the thirties building a St. Louis Democratic machine second only to Kansas City in its electoral efficiency. He had rooted out the last vestiges of the pre-1932 Republican machines in the Negro and flophouse precincts and replaced them with Democratic organizations. In the Democratic gubernatorial primary of 1940 Dickmann accomplished in St. Louis what Pendergast had done for so many years in Kansas City. As Table 9 shows, the state outside St. Louis preferred Mr. Reynolds by a narrow margin as the Democratic nominee for governor in 1940. However, a St. Louis majority of more than 70,000 votes gave

McDaniel, the Dickmann-backed candidate, a comfortable margin of victory.

TABLE 9
ST. LOUIS CITY ATTEMPTS TO RULE
1940 Democratic Gubernatorial Primary

	No. Votes for McDaniel	No. Votes for Reynolds
St. Louis City	108,117	37,687
Jackson County	52,443	50,561
Outside	162,835	165,193
Total	323,395	252,441

However, the St. Louis effort at Pendergast-style domination of state politics was ill-fated. McDaniel, the Dickmann-backed gubernatorial candidate, was defeated in the general election by Forrest Donnell, and Mayor Dickmann disappeared from the political scene when he was defeated in the St. Louis mayoralty election of 1941. Since 1941 there has been no cohesive St. Louis Democratic organization. Each ward boss has been a king unto himself. St. Louis remains important politically because it ill behooves a candidate to incur the wrath of all the ward leaders. But the city does not dominate the state as did Pendergast's Kansas City. St. Louis city has consistently supported the winning candidate since 1936, but since 1940 the pluralities reported out of St. Louis have never been greater than 20,000-25,000 in the Democratic gubernatorial primaries.

As Figure 19 indicates, however, control of the state's Democratic party has shifted from the western part of the state to the east. In Figure 18 it was the western tier of counties that voted with Pendergast and were, therefore, on the winning side from 1928

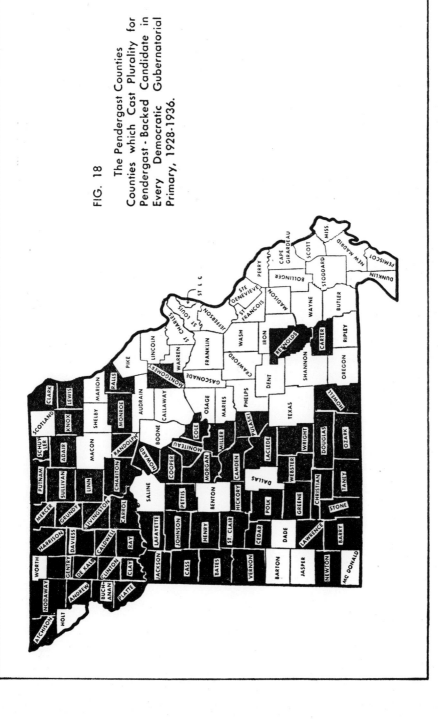

FIG. 18

The Pendergast Counties
Counties which Cast Plurality for
Pendergast - Backed Candidate in
Every Democratic Gubernatorial
Primary, 1928-1936.

through 1936. In Figure 19, however, the eastern counties are found on the winning side in every primary from 1944 through 1952.

The death of the Pendergast machine in Kansas City was the immediate precipitant of the shift of political power from west to east in the state. However, more fundamental factors were ultimately responsible. Before the New Deal the Kansas City area was the most important storehouse of Democratic votes in the state. However, since 1932 St. Louis city has changed from a Republican stronghold to a Democratic fortress. Therefore, the eastern portion of the state now outweighs the west in terms of number of Democratic votes. In addition to St. Louis city in the eastern part of the state, there are the traditionally Democratic strongholds of Little Dixie and the cotton Delta region. The most obvious outward sign of the shift in the state's center of political gravity is the unique circumstance of both United States Senators from Missouri hailing from St. Louis city.

Since 1944, no individual has exercised commanding authority in Missouri's Democratic party. Many observers describe the existing situation as chaotic. However, close examination reveals that Missouri's political scene is not so chaotic as surface appearances might indicate. A fairly cohesive group of dominant political leaders does exist in the state and these political leaders generally arrive at a consensus concerning candidates and policies in Democratic primaries.

Before entering upon a description of some of Missouri's political leaders and the reasons for their power a word of caution must be interjected. No inference should be read into what is said of an effort to portray

wily men working behind the scenes pulling the strings
of political puppets. The process by which a consensus
is reached by Missouri's political leaders is often most
informal. One political leader or a group of them will
"talk up" the merits of a person or a measure throughout the state, and thereby attempt to generate a favorable climate of opinion relative to the person or measure. In so doing, they seek out other leaders with
whom they enjoy a close association and suggest to
them that "so and so" would make a good candidate
or "such and such" a good bill. Generally, if the leaders approached have made no other commitments, and
if they have no strong feelings one way or the other,
they will accede to the request. Thereby, an organization is developed and state-wide support generated for
the prospective candidate or measure.

In 1955, some of the more important people in the
state's ruling oligarchy were: Forrest Smith, governor
from 1948 to 1952; A. D. Sappington, general counsel,
Missouri Farmers Association; Richard R. Nacy, an
official of the Central Missouri Trust Company and
a friend of President Harry S. Truman; Mike Kenney,
Jordon Chambers and Louis Berra, bosses of St.
Louis' 6th (flophouse and Negro), 18th (Negro) and
24th (Italian) wards respectively; J. B. Conrad, landowner and political leader from New Madrid in the
Delta section; Jim Pendergast, cousin of Tom Pendergast and heir to the remnants of his Kansas City
machine; Hugh Stephens, highway commissioner,
Chairman of the Board, Stephens College in Columbia,
Missouri, millionaire, civic leader, a proud bearer of
a respected "Little Dixie" name.

Forrest Smith is an important figure in Missouri

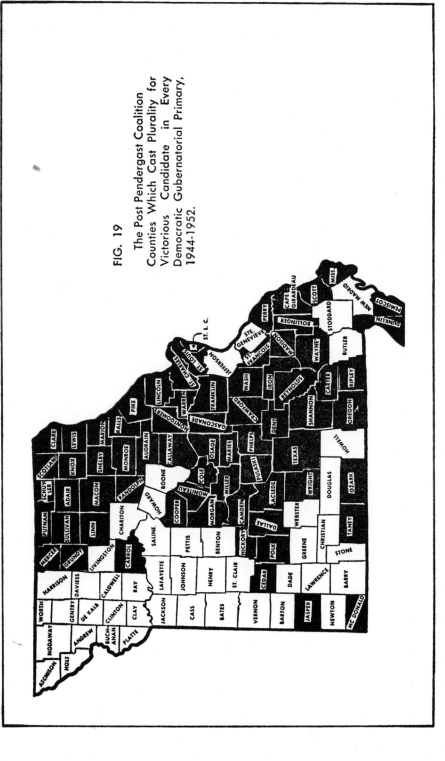

FIG. 19

The Post Pendergast Coalition Counties Which Cast Plurality for Victorious Candidate in Every Democratic Gubernatorial Primary, 1944-1952.

because of his many contacts at the county level, his likeable personality, and the prestige he enjoys because of his former occupancy of the governor's chair. Governor Smith has friends in the courthouses of the state because of his years of service as tax commissioner, a job which took him into every county of the state. In this position he was able to do many favors for many people. He has extremely close contacts in the Delta section with political leaders like J. B. Conrad. The vote of the Delta section is important because of the large pluralities which can be posted by "voting" the colored people.

A. D. Sappington possesses great power because of his position as general counsel with the most powerful and wealthy farm organization in the state, the Missouri Farmers Association, which has 150,000 members. Each month, the M.F.A.'s publicity department distributes the influential *Missouri Farmer* to all 150,000 members. In addition as a great cooperative the M.F.A. is an integral part of the state's industrial and financial community. In many of the state's counties the M.F.A. employs an attorney to act as its counsel, a practice followed by most great organizations. The persons chosen for the post are almost invariably political leaders. Sometimes they are simply local leaders; more often they are senators or representatives in the state's legislature. These people are usually susceptible to suggestions from Mr. Sappington relative to their choice of candidates in primaries and the votes they cast on key measures considered by the state legislature. Consequently, Sappington has much to offer candidates for state office in return for favors of interest to the M.F.A.

One of the paradoxes of Missouri politics is that the Missouri Farmers Association is strongest in the southwestern Ozark Republican counties and tends to support Democratic farm and labor policies, whereas the State Farm Bureau supports Republican policies and enjoys its greatest strength in Democratic counties. The reason for this paradox is that the bottom land farmers vote Democratic and the thin-soil farmers vote Republican because of tradition. However, their choice of farm organizations is dictated by direct economic considerations. The thin-soil farmer needs the advantages of a cooperative organization and thus joins the M.F.A. The well-to-do farmer, on the other hand, recognizes that Farm Bureau policies are calculated to reduce the competition of the marginal farmer and therefore joins that organization. The explicit policy point-of-view of the State Farm Bureau is that the taxpayer should not be asked to support the marginal farmer, just as he should not be required to support the marginal gasoline station operator. Thus it is in the thin-soil Republican areas of the state that Sappington enjoys his greatest influence. His authority in these counties is crucial in Democratic primaries because of the susceptibility of the low income Republican sections to organizational control in the Democratic primaries, a subject that has been ventilated at length in previous chapters.

In 1952, Sappington of the M.F.A. gave effective support to both Senator Stuart Symington and Governor P. M. Donnelly in the Democratic primary and general election. After the election of Symington and Donnelly, Sappington was appointed a highway commissioner, and Fred Heinkel, the President of the M.F.A., was appointed a trustee of the University of Missouri. Mr. Heinkel, through his University appointment, was placed in a position to snipe at the activities of University Extension people who support the Farm Bureau-backed flexible price support program and thus advance the M.F.A.'s policy points-of-view.

Another bonus enjoyed by the M.F.A. as a result of its political activity is an unusual influence over legislation offered by the governor and passed by the legislature. In one instance, the M.F.A. legislators traded with labor people, with whom its leaders have friendly relations, defeat of a "Right-to-work" bill for passage of an anti-filled milk bill. Again, in 1953, the M.F.A. requested legislation permitting them to bring grain into the state at cost for distribution to drought-stricken farmers. The governor called a special session of the legislature to deal with the problem. H. E. Kleinfelter, manager, publishing and information division of the M.F.A., wrote the governor's speech for presentation to the legislature, and Mr. Sappington drafted the necessary legislation. The bill, permitting the M.F.A. to assume control of the relief program, was speedily enacted by the legislature and signed by the governor. Thereafter, the M.F.A. was identified in the minds of Missouri's farmers with the drought relief program. Needless to say, the State Farm Bureau people derived no pleasure from the incident.

Dick Nacy of the Central Missouri Trust Company is the "moneybags" of the state's ruling oligarchy. Through his connections with the state's industrial and financial leaders, earned through his banking position, he is able to secure sizeable contributions for "acceptable" candidates. In addition, Nacy has many connections at the county level, associations which are similar in character to Sappington's. Finally, Nacy is a close personal friend of President Truman. It is said that Mr. Truman often transmits his feelings relative to candidates and programs through Nacy.

J. B. Conrad of New Madrid county has great power in southeast Missouri. His authority in the Cotton Delta section is similar to that possessed by coal operators in Kentucky and West Virginia before the New Deal. He and his fellow great landowners "vote" their tenants and Negroes as a bloc. The colored voters, it seems, are seldom burdened with the task of marking their ballots because to do so would leave the outcome unaffected.

Mike Kenney, Jordon Chambers and Louis Berra hold power in St. Louis city for the same reason that Tom Pendergast possessed it in Kansas City. They perform important services for the Negroes, immigrants and derelicts of their wards. In addition, they protect "business people" from "unnecessary" and "arbitrary" enforcement of laws. They secure licenses for tavern owners and defend the license-recipients against "arbitrary" revocation because of "minor" infractions of the city's laws. Consequently, the residents of their wards tend to vote as these leaders suggest.

Jim Pendergast of Kansas City has inherited the Tom Pendergast organization, but he is only a shadow of his famous uncle. In recent years he has more often than not found himself in opposition to the leaders of the state's Democratic party. However, a Jim Pendergast-backed candidate is usually assured of a com-

fortable majority in northwest Kansas City. Therefore, his support or opposition remains an important
factor in Democratic primaries.

Hugh Stephens, wealthy resident of Boone county in
the Little Dixie section, is a typical twentieth century
Bourbon. In many respects, he is the Bernard Baruch
of Missouri politics. Dick Nacy consults him relative
to candidates and platforms. The state's governors
often seek his opinion relative to appointments and
programs. He has long been identified with the state's
highway program and takes pride in the part he played
in "divorcing the program from politics" and placing
it in the hands of "qualified engineers." He is presently a highway commissioner and chairman of the
board of Stephens College. As a man of intellect and
integrity he commands the respect of fellow Democrats. As a millionaire, he commands the devotion of
many Little Dixie political leaders. Therefore, Hugh
Stephens' attitude toward candidates in the Democratic primaries is not taken lightly.

This description of Missouri's leading political lights
is not intended to be all-inclusive. There are many
other Democratic political figures whose support in
primaries is important. However, a prospective candidate for state-wide office must obtain the support of
some of the individuals named and/or others like them
if he is to be a serious contender in the primary.

Strength attracts strength. Therefore, support for a
candidate by one or more of the political leaders
named tends to polarize constantly increasing attention and support around the favored candidate. In
some instances, support is obtained through solicita-
tion by a candidate. In other cases, a number of

political leaders will meet and discuss possible candidates for the forthcoming election. All those present will propose names. As the names are presented, objections will be raised, such as "He's too closely identified with labor," or "He's been involved in a number of questionable enterprises or affairs." Finally, someone might hit on a name to which few objections can be interposed; for example, that of Stuart Symington in 1952. Comments such as, "He's a businessman, but has a good labor record" and "He can carry both Little Dixie and St. Louis city" might meet the presentation of a name such as Symington's.

If a consensus is reached one member of the group may be assigned the task of "sounding out" the prospective candidate. When the prospective candidate agrees to enter the race, the political leaders concerned contact other leaders, such as Forrest Smith, Hugh Stephens, Dick Nacy and Jim Pendergast. Some of the leaders contacted may agree to support the candidate, others may demur. However, the compulsion to join the ranks of the candidate accelerates as his strength increases. It is important to a politician or an interest group leader to be on the winning side and at an early date. The early aid is the most decisive in a candidate's campaign, and a newly elected governor can be expected to reward his earliest supporters most generously.

In Missouri the process of consensus and polarization is informal and involves a great many people, both in and out of government. As a result, promises must be made to many individuals and groups before decisive support can be obtained for a candidate.

Economic Divisions

Missouri's Democratic party is not afflicted with social and economic divisions of the same magnitude which characterize Kentucky and West Virginia's Democratic party. As already indicated, the principal divisions within the party revolve around centers of political strength, such as Pendergast's Kansas City machine, rather than economic groupings.

There are three primary reasons for the relative absence of economic factionalism in the state's Democratic party. In the first place, the business community as an economic group takes little part in Democratic primaries, apart from the activities of individuals who seek special privileges. This is due to the twin facts that 1) most businessmen as individuals are in the Republican party; and 2) the state's governor is a "weak" executive who is in no position to disturb the state's established economic and social order. Therefore, the tendency of the business community has been to "leave politics to the politicians." In the second place, the Little Dixie Bourbons have almost always occupied a prominent place in the councils of the party and, therefore, have rarely opposed the party's nominee as a unified group. Thirdly, organized labor represents no immediate threat to the prevailing balance of power in the party. Labor has neither the necessary vote, nor, seemingly, the desire to dominate the state's Democratic party.

However, on the rare occasions when the ruling groups of the state have felt their hegemony threatened, a social and economic division of the electorate has resulted comparable to that observed in Kentucky and

West Virginia. Two such elections occurred at the turn of the century, in 1896 and 1908.

In the election of 1896, rural Missouri rallied to the banner of William Jennings Bryan as befitted the home of Silver Dick Bland. The greatest gains enjoyed by the Democratic party in that election were in the impoverished Republican Ozark highlands. This was Dick Bland's congressional district and years of indoctrination had prepared the voters to follow silver in preference to tradition.

The difference between the reaction of the Ozark people and that of their Kentucky and West Virginia mountain cousins to Bryan's candidacy is striking. In Kentucky and West Virginia's mountain counties Bryan's vote was lower, proportionately, than was Cleveland's in 1892. In Missouri, however, it was the increased Democratic vote in the poor Republican Ozark counties that balanced the defection of the urban centers from the Democratic ranks in 1896, and left Missouri safely in the Democratic camp.

It is interesting to reflect upon some of the possible reasons for the vote given Bryan by the Ozark section of Missouri as compared to the decreased Democratic pluralities which were returned in Kentucky and West Virginia's sister mountain sections in 1896. The predominant variable was probably organization. The Farmers Alliance had succeeded in organizing most of the Ozark Republican counties. When the election was held the pro-silver Ozark people voted, and when the votes were counted they made certain that their votes were included in the total and in the proper column. Louis Brownlow tells in his *A Passion for*

Politics, An Autobiography, of the heroic measures necessary in Dallas county, a Republican stronghold in the Missouri Ozarks, to assure an honest count of the ballots. According to Brownlow, approximately one hundred Bryan supporters marched on the county seat the dawn of election day and forced the authorities to give the "silver" Democrats positions as election judges and clerks.[1]

In Kentucky and West Virginia the mountain counties were never well organized by the silver people, and when the votes were counted in 1896 it was the professional politicians who announced the decision. Once again, the importance of the organizational level in political campaigns is made apparent. In Kentucky and West Virginia, as in Missouri, an appeal was made to men's minds on behalf of the issues of 1896. But in Kentucky and West Virginia the votes cast for Bryan were often discarded because the Bryan supporters were not well organized, whereas in Missouri, the silver Democrats assured an honest count of the ballots cast by demanding a part in the crucial counting process.

Another of Missouri's electoral contests in which a measureable division along economic lines occurred, took place in 1908. Before entering upon a discussion of that contest it is necessary to travel backward in time to 1904 when Joe Folk, the crusading St. Louis circuit attorney, was nominated and elected governor. In that same year, the Republicans carried the state in a presidential election for the first time since 1872, and carried every major state office except that of

---

[1] Louis Brownlow, *A Passion for Politics, An Autobiography,* (University of Chicago Press, 1955), pp. 158-160.

governor. One reason for the success of the Republican ticket in 1904 was undoubtedly the presence of a gold Democrat on the national ticket. However, another important reason was the disastrous (for the Democrats) effect Joe Folk's revelations of corruption in the city of St. Louis and in the state had upon both public opinion in rural Missouri and upon the Democratic machine in St. Louis.

During his administration as governor, Folk earned nationwide fame for his trust-busting activities. Oil companies, railroads, great corporations were investigated and taken to court by Folk's crusading Republican Attorney General, Hadley. In 1908, Folk sought nomination as United States Senator. This was the first year in which the nomination of candidates became a function, theoretically, of the people. Folk was defeated in the Democratic primary by some 15,000 votes out of a total cast of more than 300,000.

Folk carried 77 of the state's 115 counties. However, the counties he lost represented the areas of concentrated Democratic strength. He lost eight of the "Little Dixie" counties, both Kansas City and St. Louis city, and most of the relatively wealthy heavily populated counties along the Missouri River. The counties Folk carried were the more rural, less wealthy, and less heavily populated counties of the state.

Thus the split between pro and anti-Folk forces represented an economic division of the electorate. The forces that opposed Folk were the business community and the Democratic leadership. The railroads and other corporate enterprises had become bitter enemies of Folk by the time his four-year term as governor had been completed because of the investigations of corporate practices he initiated and the regulatory legislation he supported. Many Democratic leaders felt that Folk had destroyed the party by his indiscriminate investigations into political corruption. Therefore, in the wealthier sections of the state, which are also areas of Democratic strength, the Democratic leaders were not averse to helping the business community in their efforts to destroy Folk. The Folk primary was the last political division in the Democratic primary along economic lines in Missouri. From the Folk primary and until 1956, the fundamental intraparty division has been between the eastern and western sections of the state.

Conclusions

Missouri's chief executive is a "weak" governor. His power is not sufficient to enable him to lead his party. Therefore, party control tends to lodge in the hands of individuals who control a large block of votes or combinations of local leaders and people representing powerful interest groups. As a result, the governor of the state is often obligated to a coalition of political leaders and special interest leaders for his election. At other times, the governor may be forced to pay homage to individual leaders, such as Tom Pendergast.

The most important clash of interests in Missouri has been between St. Louis and Kansas City. During the period of Pendergast's domination of state politics, the western portion of the state was dominant in the party. Since 1940, when Pendergast suffered the lash of reform, the eastern portion of the state has assumed a dominant position in the politics of the state. The reasons for the shift in the state's center of political gravity are: 1) the destruction of the Pendergast machine in Kansas City; and 2) the emergence of St. Louis city as a Democratic stronghold.

Fundamentally, Missouri's political pattern is similar to that of the other Border States. However, because the Bourbons do not rule in Missouri, although they have enjoyed a continuing position of considerable influence within the party, no Bourbon-liberal split has developed in Missouri comparable to those observed in Kentucky and West Virginia. In the absence of a polarization around a Bourbon-liberal issue, or around a central source of organizational strength such as an Administration or Statehouse group, the polarization has been around concentrations of voting strength and wealth.

CHAPTER VII

MISSOURI TRENDS

THE COMPOSITION of Missouri's population has undergone steady change since the Civil War. The changing composition of the state's population has been a determining factor in terms of party structure, i.e., political organization and factionalism. The population changes responsible for the type of party structure in the state have had an equally profound effect on the composition of the two political parties and on their relative strength. Of interest, then, is the amount, locus and causes of political change as it has taken place in Missouri.

The Background

The fundamental structure of Missouri politics is a product of geography and population movements. The initial population movement into the state came largely from the Upper South, and was composed of many slaveholders who settled primarily along the rivers and in the more fertile sections of the state adjacent to or near the rivers. Later population movements stemmed in large part from the north, and tended to settle in the less populated sections of the state, in the northwest and southwest corners of the state. Therefore, the areas settled earliest, by Southerners, and which are also the more fertile, tend to be Democratic; and those settled later, by Northerners, and which are largely thin soil sections tend to be Republican.

Exceptions to this generalization are found in some river counties and the western Ozarks section. Many river counties, though settled at an early date by Southerners, have become predominantly Republican because of the Republican-inclined German population which has since settled there. The western Ozarks section, which was also settled at an early date by mountain people from the Upper South, is also Republican; the reason being that Missouri's mountain folk, like their brethren in Kentucky and West Virginia, have been stalwart Republicans since the Civil War. In addition, there was a considerable influx of people from northern states into the Ozarks following the Civil War, and this new population was largely Republican.

Figure 20 identifies the centers of strength of the two principal political parties. Reference to the figure discloses that there are five major centers of Democratic strength and three of Republican dominance in the state. The Democrats are the majority party in 1) the southeastern Missouri cotton-growing lowlands (the Delta section); 2) the eastern Ozarks, Maries county south and east to the Arkansas border; 3) Jackson county (Kansas City) and five counties immediately north of it; 4) the so-called "Little Dixie" area in central and northeastern Missouri; and 5) St. Louis city.

Republican strength is concentrated in 1) the southwestern Ozark region; 2) the corn belt in northern and northwestern Missouri; and 3) the "German Belt," beginning on the west with Lafayette and Carroll counties and extending along the southern reaches of the Missouri River to the St. Louis area and continuing south along the Mississippi to the cotton counties.

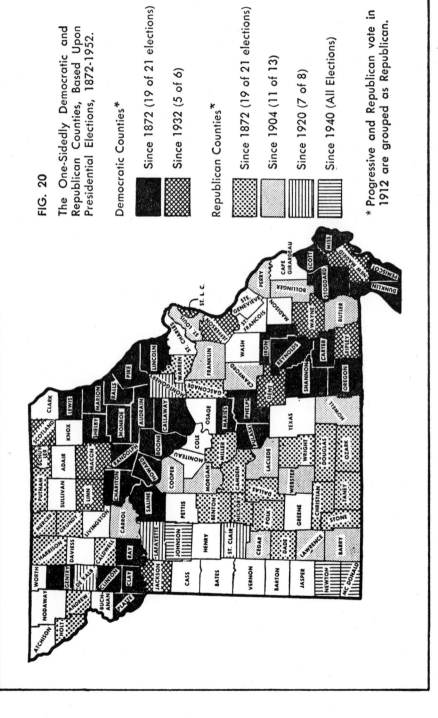

FIG. 20

The One-Sidedly Democratic and Republican Counties, Based Upon Presidential Elections, 1872-1952.

Democratic Counties*

Since 1872 (19 of 21 elections)

Since 1932 (5 of 6)

Republican Counties*

Since 1872 (19 of 21 elections)

Since 1904 (11 of 13)

Since 1920 (7 of 8)

Since 1940 (All Elections)

* Progressive and Republican vote in 1912 are grouped as Republican.

Political Change in Missouri

Figure 21 identifies the direction of the political change that has occurred in Missouri over the period 1916-1952. The figure shows that the political change that has occurred in the state has a distinct sectional cast. The eastern portion of the state has registered, with but few exceptions, a plus Democratic trend since 1916. However, the western part of the state is even more unanimous in its plus Republican tendencies. Only five western Missouri counties have seen Democratic gains, and four of the five western counties showing a plus Democratic change contain the larger cities of the state; i.e., in Greene county is the city of Springfield with a 1950 population of 66,302; in Jackson county, Kansas City with a population of 453,290; in Jasper county, Joplin with a population of 75,572; and Buchanan county contains St. Joseph with a population of 75,572. These four cities are among the six largest in the state.

Recent political change in Missouri has been centered around four variables: 1) population change; 2) the differential impact of certain events and governmental policies on various elements of the population; 3) the rise of the cities, the formation of powerful machines therein, and the periodic decline of the political machines; and 4) a political variable which might be classified as "organization" or the lack of it. Other variables might be listed, but these four seem to be of primary importance in explaining the political change that has occurred in the state.

1. Population Change

The population movements which have occurred in the state represent one of the principal reasons for the

east-west pattern of Missouri's political change. The
initial population movement into Missouri stemmed
primarily from the Upper South. The people entering
the state from the Upper South traveled largely by
way of the rivers and upon arrival in Missouri tended
to settle along the banks of their medium of transport.
It was along the Mississippi and Missouri Rivers that
they originally constructed their homesteads. Gradually these people moved up into the area now known
as "Little Dixie." Interestingly enough, the lowlanders
from the Upper South settled along the rivers and in
the Little Dixie section, and the highlanders sought
out the crags and streams of southwestern Missouri.

Therefore, in 1850 the population of Missouri was
almost identical to that of the Upper South. However,
after 1850 and until the present date great changes
have taken place in the composition of Missouri's
population. One of the more important aspects of the
population change that has occurred is the increase
in the proportion of Missouri's population hailing
from the North Central states. Included in this North
Central group are Kansas, Nebraska, and Iowa, all
bordering Missouri on the west and north. In 1850,
none of those residing in Missouri was born in
Kansas; in 1950, 125,830 residents had moved from
the Jayhawker state to Missouri. In 1950, 26,205
Nebraskans lived in Missouri compared to none in
1850. And Iowans accounted for 57,510 members of
the Missouri population in 1950 compared to 1,366
in 1850. Politically speaking, the important thing about
the new population is that most of it is Republican by
tradition and conviction.

Most of the influx of population from western states

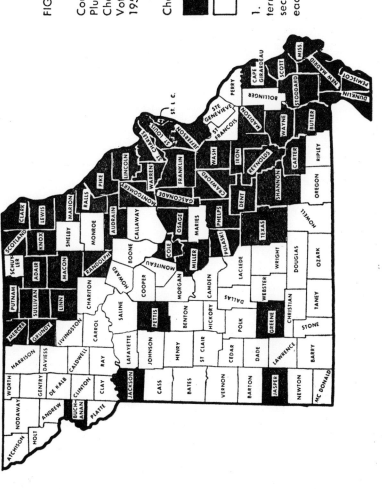

FIG. 21

Political Change

Counties by Plus Democratic or Plus Republican Percentage-Point Change in Percent of Two-Party Vote, Presidential Elections, 1916-1952.

Change:

■ Plus Democratic Change

□ Plus Republican Change

1. Political change is measured in terms of a line of regression or secular trend line computed for each county.

found homes in the western part of the state. A population movement has certain similarities to the deposition of soil by a stream of water. When a torrent of water streams out of the sky, the unprotected soil is washed away and deposited wherever the water slows, the layers of new soil thinning downstream from the point at which the water's movement is slowed. The emigration of people from the farms of a state like Kansas is similar in kind to the movement of their soil. In Kansas there have been depressions, dust storms and droughts which have swept people from their farms. The population rush away from these disasters slowed as it reached the relatively fertile land and prosperous cities of western Missouri, and was deposited near the state line, with thinner layers to be found east of the line. Concentrations of the new population are located along lines of communications such as rivers and railroad lines (note the spearhead of plus Republican change in Figure 21 extending along the Missouri River to Callaway county).

Therefore, the tendency of counties in the western part of the state and along the Missouri River to become more Republican is largely explicable in terms of population change. Many Kansans and Iowans have sold their farms and bought land in the Osage Plains area south of Jackson county, including the counties of Cass, Bates, Vernon, Barton, Jackson, Henry, St. Clair, Cedar, Dade, Benton and Pettis. Pettis county, which has registered a plus Democratic change since 1916, differs from the other counties of the Osage Plains group in the per cent of its population which is urban. Pettis county contains the city of Sedalia and is 65% urban, compared with

a high of 35% among the ten other counties of the
Osage Plains section. However, Pettis county outside
Sedalia has registered a plus Republican change com-
parable to that of the more rural counties of the Osage
Plains (see Figure 22). The pattern of political change
in Pettis county is remarkably similar to that observed
in Kentucky's Fayette county (see for comparison
Figure 13).

Most of the counties in the eastern section of Missouri, unlike the western counties, have registered a
plus Democratic change since 1916. Population-wise,
the eastern counties differ from the western in that
they have absorbed an increasing influx of population
from the Deep South, and a still larger though diminishing influx from the Upper South. This new population is largely Democratic in character.

The Cotton Delta region in extreme southeast Missouri has experienced the most pronounced plus Democratic change in the state and also the most profound
population change. Thad Snow, a resident of Mississippi county in the Cotton Delta during the twenties,
describes in his book, *From Missouri,* the type of population change that occurred in the Delta region. According to Thad Snow, the Delta region was Northern
before 1924, both in terms of its culture and its
economy. Most of the population consisted of land-
seekers from the middle west, and the most important
crop was wheat. But in the short space of the first
few months of 1924, the Delta became Southern. The
reason was the boll weevil, which had pretty well de-
pleted the cotton crop south of the Delta. Therefore,
in search of land that would grow cotton, the Southern
black belt cotton growers invaded and conquered the

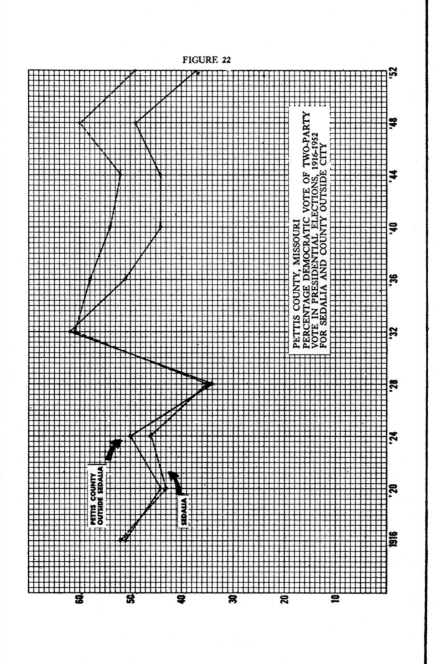

FIGURE 22

PETTIS COUNTY, MISSOURI
PERCENTAGE DEMOCRATIC VOTE OF TWO-PARTY
VOTE IN PRESIDENTIAL ELECTIONS, 1916-1952
FOR SEDALIA AND COUNTY OUTSIDE CITY

section. According to Snow, approximately ten thousand Negro share croppers moved into the Delta in the first two months of 1924. Prior to that date, Negroes were a rarity in the section.[1]

Politically, the effect of the influx of people from the South into southeast Missouri was revolutionary. Overnight, the counties of the Delta section were changed from politically marginal locales into strongholds of the Democratic faith. In 1918, C. O. Sauer opined in the *American Political Science Review* that the Delta region was about to become a Republican stronghold because of the influx of corn and wheat farmers from the middle west.[2] Not six years after he made this fully justifiable prediction the area had become almost as strongly Democratic as any black belt section in the state of Mississippi, proving the perils inherent in political predictions.

2. *The Differential Impact of Events and Governmental Policies*

The events having the most important impact on the Missouri political scene have been: 1) the Civil War, 2) the gold-silver controversy, 3) World War I, 4) the Great Depression, and 5) World War II.

The Civil War is responsible for the basic configuration of the Missouri political map. The rich farming areas along the Missouri and Mississippi rivers were originally settled by Southern slaveholders who became strongly Democratic following the Civil War, and their ancestors remain so inclined. However, the German influx of population also followed the rivers

---

[1] Thad Snow, *From Missouri*, (Boston, 1954), pp. 144-157.
[2] C. O. Sauer, "Geography and the Gerrymander," *American Political Science Review*, Vol. 12, (August, 1918), p. 412.

and the Germans were strongly pro-Union during the Civil War and inclined Republican thereafter.

In many instances the long-term effect of a given pattern of population change is not immediately apparent. In the case of the Germans and the Negroes, for example, it was not the population movement as such which precipitated political change, but rather the subsequent events which have led them to favor either the Democratic or Republican party.

It is widely believed in Missouri that the German population of Missouri, led by Carl Schurz, saved Missouri for the Union. After the Civil War, the Germans tended to support the Republican party in opposition to the states-rights Democratic forces. Since the Civil War, an accumulation of circumstances have led the German population to identify their interests even more closely with those of the Republican party. First, because most Germans settled in the cities and engaged in mercantile and industrial persuits, they found Republican policies relative to the money question and tariffs to their liking. Secondly, coincidentally with Democratic administrations America has participated in two world wars in opposition to Germany. In both these conflicts the American Germans were subject to suspicion and some outright persecution.

Lafayette county provides an example of the effect two wars with Germany have had on Democratic fortunes in counties with large German populations. Before 1920, Lafayette county was classified politically and culturally with the Little Dixie counties. It had been invariably Democratic in both local and national elections since the Civil War. Herbert Bates, state treasurer and resident of Lafayette county, recalls what happened in the county in 1920. According to Mr. Bates, "Every German in the county who was eligible to vote and could walk, crawl, or be carried to the polls marked his ballot on that November day in 1920. The result was not only a Republican victory in 1920, but a permanent transference of the county to the Republican column." This scene was repeated throughout the state in counties with sizeable German populations. Again, in 1940, when President Roosevelt expressed his antagonism to Naziism in unrestrained language, the German Republican counties in the St. Louis area reacted in the 1940 general election by returning markedly increased pluralities for Republican candidates. It was this change, in combination with the Pendergast downfall, that was responsible for the precipitous decline in the state's percentage Democratic vote in 1940, and the election of a Republican governor.

The single event since the Civil War which caused Germans to search their Republican souls was prohibition and the Rooseveltian-backed repeal of that much-maligned piece of legislation. The art of brewing is a proud and lucrative German pursuit, and its death in 1919 was a cruel blow. Therefore, many St. Louis brewery owners have become steadfast Democrats and lend their money and prestige to the Democratic party when the occasion demands. Germans further removed from St. Louis city, however, were less affected by prohibition and repeal, and largely remain devoted to the Republican party.

The Negro population of Missouri is the only homogeneous population group, other than the German, that has undergone profound political change as a result of recent events and political policies. Missouri's Negroes, like colored people elsewhere, voted Republican, where they were permitted to exercise the franchise, until 1932. The Roosevelt revolution worked the same magic on the colored vote in Missouri as elsewhere. The two places wherein the percentage increase in the state's Negro population has been greatest are St. Louis city and the Cotton Delta section in southeast Missouri. These are also the two places wherein the percentage-point increase in Democratic vote has been greatest since 1916.

The Little Dixie section in northeast Missouri is the only area outside St. Louis city, Kansas City, and the Cotton Delta, containing a large Negro population. However, the Little Dixie section's percentage Negro population has suffered a steady decline. The principal reason for the percentage decline of Little Dixie's Negro population is that corn and wheat farming predominate, a type of farming requiring a minimum of unskilled farm labor. The Little Dixie section's moderate increase in the percentage of its vote cast for Democratic candidates may be explained, in part, by the new political orientation of the colored vote. The relatively minor impact on Little Dixie of the change in colored voting habits may be attributed to the fact that colored people have never voted in great numbers in the section.

Missouri's business, labor, and farm communities have also been alternately attracted to and repelled from one or the other of the two major political parties as a result of various events, and the policies of the two political parties relative to those events.

In Missouri, the urban business community was

alienated from the Democratic party at the turn of the century by the party's easy money policies. Some small business people supported the efforts of rural confederates to obtain legislation regulating railroads, because they, too, suffered from the discriminatory practices of the carriers. However, after the desired regulatory legislation was passed they found that they had little in common with the confederates and have tended to vote Republican. The New Deal period confirmed the suspicions of the business community concerning the Democratic party. Outstate, however, the political orientation of members of the business community generally conforms to the political habits of the area in which they reside. Most banking and business people in the Little Dixie area are Democratic. On the other hand, their brethren in the Ozark section are Republican.

The farmers of Missouri represent a more complex subject for study than either the business or labor communities. The Populist movement induced many farmers who were traditionally Republican to enter the Democratic ranks. The election of 1896 was as revolutionary as the Civil War in disrupting traditional political patterns. However, the candidacy of Parker, the gold Democrat, in 1904, restored the Missouri political scene to much the same expression it had worn since the Civil War. The only residual change was the loss of business support by the Democratic party. The elections of 1932 and 1936 once again saw a political realignment in favor of the Democrats in the rural Ozarks and northern Missouri. Since 1940, however, Republican farm sections have returned with even greater enthusiasm to the Republican column with augmented pluralities for its candidates.

The Delta section's pronounced plus Democratic trend presents a decided contrast to the plus Republican trend of the thin soil areas. The political behavior of the Delta counties is due to the grateful response of the cotton farmers to New Deal farm policies as well as to population change. The cotton farmers of the Delta credit the New Deal with saving their farms. Republican thin soil farmers, however, complain that they have benefited less from New Deal farm policies than have the more substantial farmers. In addition, the thin soil farmers look askance at the loss of "freedom" and "initiative" which many feel attends such measures as relief and price supports.

However, the actions of thin soil farmers often belie their words. The Missouri Farmers Association is the strongest farm organization in the Republican western Ozarks, and leaders of the M.F.A. feel that they are articulating the sentiment of their membership when they give uncompromising support to a rigid 100 per cent of parity support program. M.F.A. officials explain the lack of support for Democratic farm policies among thin soil Republican farmers to a failure on the farmers' part to identify "liberal" farm measures with the Democratic party. In the minds of Republican farmers, the Democratic party is synonymous with "Bourbon" and "rebel." They identify "liberal" farm legislation with people such as Norris and Borah and LaFollette, all Republicans. The Republican thin soil farmers are not as conservative as they sound, according to some M.F.A. people.

In Missouri, as in Kentucky and West Virginia,

organized labor has responded gratefully to New Deal policies. Some of the Democratic party's greatest gains in cities such as St. Louis have occurred in wards with a large labor population. The reasons for organized labor's support for Democratic policies are identical to those cited for labor's support in West Virginia, i.e., increased political and economic bargaining power as a result of various New Deal policies.

3. Political Organization, the Rise of the Cities, and Reform

At the turn of the century, the concentrated and growing population of the cities was assuming a new importance. Ed Butler's St. Louis machine had become a keystone in the arch of Democratic rule. The Butler machine was important for several reasons. First, it provided the ruling clique with an easily controlled bloc of votes in conventions; and secondly, it provided them with a source of Democratic votes in general elections that could fluctuate in harmony with the needs of the moment. Folk's destruction of the Butler machine upset the balance of power within the Democratic party and helped turn the state from a Democratic stronghold into a marginal state.

The body blow delivered to Tom Pendergast's Kansas City machine in 1940 also had a deleterious effect on Democratic fortunes in the state. Before the death of the Pendergast machine, Kansas City regularly returned majorities in excess of 60 per cent for Democratic party candidates. Since 1940, Kansas City's Democratic majorities have hovered nearer the 50 per cent mark. However, even more important than the loss of Kansas City votes was the loss of leadership which attended the political disappearance of Pendergast. There was no longer an individual who decided that "this is the man we'll support," and then generated the enthusiasm necessary to nominate and elect the chosen man.

Perhaps the loss of western leadership in the Democratic party when Pendergast disappeared behind bars is as responsible for the plus Republican change that has occurred in western Missouri as population change. It is interesting to compare Figure 21 showing the areas of plus Republican change with Figure 18 which identifies the counties in which the Pendergast organization was dominant. Virtually every county in the first category is also in the second. The correlation is not a matter of coincidence. After 1940, the leaders in the Pendergast-controlled counties no longer had the same incentive to "get out and work" at election time. Perhaps most of them still hope for a Democratic victory, but it is now just a wish rather than a drive kept burning by visions of gold and glory.

One other factor in political change deserves to be mentioned. The *Kansas City Star* (Kansas City is a one-newspaper town) enjoys its greatest circulation precisely in the area where a considerable plus Republican trend has taken place. This paper has made the name "Democratic" synonymous with the value adjective "machine" in its columns. In fact, as the *Star* sees it, in local elections the contest is never between a Democrat and a Reform or Republican candidate, but between a tool of the "machine" and a "citizens" nominee. Inevitably, this style of presentation of political issues has had an impact on the political attitudes of the rural as well as the urban subscribers to the paper. The good Baptists and Methodists of rural Missouri have always regarded Kansas City as a den of vice and iniquity. In recent years, the den's iniquity has been identified with the noun "Democrat."

Conclusions

The rise of the cities has had a striking effect on Missouri's political scene. While Pendergast's Kansas City machine was dominant the western part of the state tended to dominate the party. Now that the Kansas City machine is dead the eastern section rules the Democratic forces, largely because of the resurgence of Democratic strength in St. Louis city. The absence of effective organizational efforts in western Missouri since 1940 has helped produce a plus Republican trend, whereas the new vigor imparted to Democratic forces in the east has helped bring about a plus Democratic trend in that area.

The organizational variable, however, is only one factor among many. The fact that Democrats from the South tend to enter eastern Missouri, whereas Republicans from the West tend to enter Missouri from the west is also an important determinant in bringing about the type of political change observed in these areas.

Recent events and policy pronouncements of the two political parties have also played a part in changing the political spectrum. However, it is only among the Negroes and Germans that this variable has had a striking effect. The Civil War and two wars with Germany are the events which have made Republicans of most Germans. Release from slavery by Abraham Lincoln made Republicans of most Negroes until 1932,

when Franklin Roosevelt emerged as a latter-day
emancipator.

The rural populace reacts less vigorously to events
and political policies than do other portions of the
population. In most cases, catastrophic events and
policy pronouncements are used by the rural folk to
rationalize whatever political faith they might have
inherited. However, a great depression or an important
economic issue can occasionally produce tremendous
changes in voting behavior. Since the Civil War, however, these shifts in voting behavior have always been
followed by a return to the faith of their fathers, unless
accompanied by population change.

CHAPTER VIII

POLITICAL ORGANIZATION AND
FACTIONALISM IN MARYLAND

BASICALLY, the story of factionalism and political organization in Maryland is uncomplicated. There are two Democratic parties in the state. One is located in Baltimore city, the other in Tidewater Maryland.

Prior to 1932 the Baltimore city Democratic party was controlled by the business community. Since 1932, the manipulable vote of the city has been lost to the business community and has come, increasingly, under the sway of the great labor organizations. Thus the Democratic party of the city is the party of labor and the liberals.

The Tidewater Maryland Democratic party is a direct descendant of the slaveowner's Whig party. The people of the section did not join the Democratic party out of devotion to the principles of Jefferson, but because of their antipathy to the party of Lincoln and abolition. Consequently, the Democratic party of the Tidewater section is the party of white supremacy and the conservatives.

Before 1932, it was not difficult for the conservative business community Democrats in Baltimore city and the Bourbons of southern Maryland to resolve differences concerning candidates and policies. Therefore, the Democratic party, at the state level, was relatively strong and unified. Since the New Deal, however, the

Baltimore city Democratic party has increasingly
become the party of the New Deal, rather than the
party of Grover Cleveland. The resultant strains and
stresses on the fabric of the party have been under-
standably great.

The true center of gravity of the Democratic party
outside Baltimore city is in the Eastern Shore counties
of Tidewater Maryland. The Eastern Shore is generally defined as Cecil and the counties south ranging
along the eastern side of Chesapeake Bay down to
Somerset and Worcester counties. After the Civil
War the colored vote was effectively neutralized in
most of the Eastern Shore counties and the area has
been a Democratic stronghold since that date. However, the colored vote in combination with that of
white Republicans captured the county governments
in some of the Tidewater counties after the Civil War
and many of these counties remain Republican strongholds. Notable among these are Charles and Calvert
on the Western Shore, and Dorchester and Somerset
counties on the Eastern Shore.

The western Maryland hill and farm people are
largely Republicans, for much the same reasons that
the West Virginia, Kentucky, and Missouri hill folk
are Republican-inclined. The people of the section
had few slaves at the time of the Civil War, and were
pro-Union during the war. In addition, many of the
early settlers of western Maryland were from northern
states.

Maryland's political configuration has produced a
Democratic party leadership which stems largely from

Baltimore city and the Eastern Shore section and which tries awkwardly to work in harness. Republican party leadership is centered principally in Baltimore city and western Maryland, a combination which has fewer policy differences than does the Democratic party leadership. The story of the process by which these coalitions attempt to nominate and elect candidates for office revolves around political organization and the economic and social intra-party divisions which complicate political organization. In order to understand Maryland's political structure it is necessary to concentrate almost exclusively upon the state's Democratic party, because it is in the contradictions within the Democratic party that can be found the reasons for increasing Republican strength in the state.

Political Organization

Democratic political organization in Maryland has much in common with the other Border States examined. In the first place, the personalities in the "organization" consist largely of professional politicians who are primarily interested in electing candidates to office. Consequently, the "organization" in Maryland, as in Kentucky, West Virginia, and Missouri, acts as a bridge between the social and economic divisions within the party. In the second place, the "organization" as an entity independent of the social and economic groupings within the party receives most of its electoral support in Democratic primaries from the largely Republican Western Shore and western mountain sections, and from the lower socio-economic

Fourth Legislative District in Baltimore city [1] (see Figure 23 showing counties which have been carried consistently by the organization in Democratic primaries, 1934-1954). These are sections of Maryland which are susceptible to organization control in Democratic primaries for the same reason that the vote of Kentucky's Eastern Mountains, Missouri's Ozarks, and West Virginia's "Hardhead" Ohio River Republican sections are controlled by their states' Democratic "organization" in Democratic primaries; i.e., dependence of Deomcratic politicians in Republican counties on the organization's patronage and related plums.

The objective of Maryland's Democratic "organization," as of all political organizations, is to nominate

---

[1] Figure 23 leaves the impression that Baltimore city has opposed the candidacy of the organization candidates in two of the six Democratic gubernatorial primary elections over the period 1934-1954. This is true in terms of total vote, but not entirely true in terms of the Legislative District Unit Vote. In terms of Legislative District Unit vote, the organization carried the Fourth Legislative District in every primary during the period.

Maryland's unique County and Legislative District Unit law applies only to party primaries. The *Maryland Manual* describes the state's County Unit law as follows:

> The individual receiving the greatest unit vote at the State Convention is the nominee of the party. Nominations are decided on the unit basis for the offices of United States Senator, Governor, Comptroller, and Attorney-General. Each County and Legislative District of Baltimore City is entitled to a unit vote equal to the number of members of the House of Delegates and the State Senate who represent the county or district. Each unit vote is cast for the individual receiving the greatest number of popular votes in the particular county or Legislative District represented.

Baltimore city has six Legislative Districts under the terms of the law, with six representatives and one senator from each District in the General Assembly. Therefore, in a party nominating convention the total vote cast by the city is 42, out of a total state vote of 152. The percentage of the total county unit vote cast by Baltimore city is 28 per cent, whereas the registered Democratic voters of Baltimore city represent 44 per cent of the total Democratic registrants in the state (1950).

Because of the County Unit system it is possible for a primary candidate to receive a minority of the total vote cast and still win the contest. And because of the division of Baltimore city into six Legislative Districts it is possible for a candidate to carry the city by a sizeable majority and still lose a portion of its Unit vote.

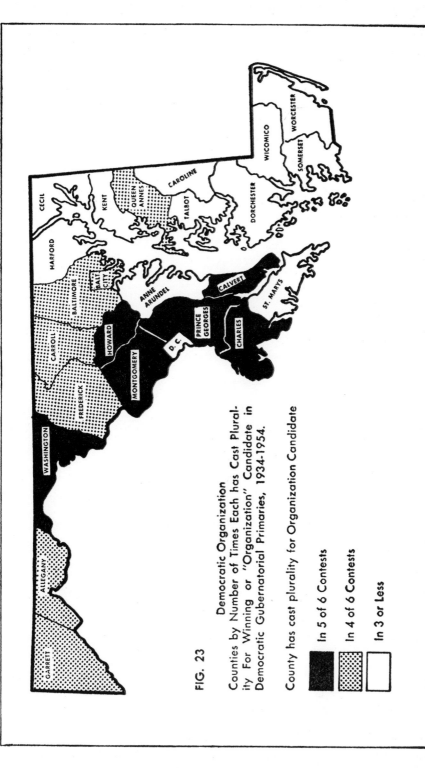

FIG. 23

Democratic Organization

Counties by Number of Times Each has Cast Plurality For Winning or "Organization" Candidate in Democratic Gubernatorial Primaries, 1934-1954.

County has cast plurality for Organization Candidate

In 5 of 6 Contests

In 4 of 6 Contests

In 3 or Less

candidates who have a chance of being elected. This means nominating candidates who can carry Baltimore city without gagging the Eastern Shore. And the means available to the organization in attempting to nominate such candidates is the organization vote in the Republican counties and the lower socio-economic Fourth Legislative District.

The *modus operandi* of the Democratic party's dominant coalition or "organization" is well illustrated by the 1946 primary. In that contest, W. Preston Lane was the organization candidate. He was a candidate whom the laboring people of Baltimore city could support in the general election, but still was not overly repugnant to the more conservative element of southern Maryland. Preston Lane was a typical Border State Democratic candidate. As a banker, an industrialist, and the possessor of a proud Maryland name, he could depend upon a good deal of conservative Democratic support. And, on the other hand, as a loyal organization Democrat with a record of consistent support for national candidates of the Democratic party he could rely upon support from labor and the liberals.

However, in January of 1946, Representative H. Streett Baldwin of suburban Baltimore county made a bid for the Democratic gubernatorial nomination in opposition to Lane with a blistering attack on the CIO Political Action Committee. Shortly thereafter, Baldwin found the reaction in the Tidewater counties to his anti-P.A.C. outburst encouraging enough to prompt him to file for the nomination. National Representative Sasscer (an arch-conservative Democrat) of southern Maryland's Western Shore immediately announced his support of Baldwin's candidacy, followed by other conservative Western Shore Democratic political leaders, such as Philip M. Dorsey, Jr., of St. Mary's county, who championed this "unafraid" opponent of communism and the C.I.O.-P.A.C.

Representative Baldwin was not a recent convert to the conservative position. While a United States Representative (1942-1946), Baldwin consistently aligned himself with the Southern conservative wing of the Democratic party. For example, in the 79th Congress, Baldwin voted to kill price and rent controls, generally opposed the school lunch program, cast his vote in support of the Case labor bill which the labor movement opposed, and either voted against or absented himself in roll calls on civil rights bills.[1]

In addition to the support generated for Baldwin in the Western Shore section, signs began to multiply that Baldwin would almost certainly carry the Eastern Shore in a two-way contest. Lane suffered from two significant disabilities in the Eastern Shore counties. In the first place, he had been attorney general during Governor Ritchie's 1930-1934 administration, when, in 1931, the governor directed his attorney general to "pry into" a lynching that occurred in Wicomico county on the Eastern Shore. This unheard of interference in local affairs, in clear violation of the sacred tenets of the much-revered Thomas Jefferson, was greatly resented by the local (white) inhabitants. In the second place, Lane, because of his support of the national ticket was vulnerable to charges of fraternization with the much-reviled C.I.O.-P.A.C. In the 1944 campaign he had served as state Democratic campaign

---

[1] *New Republic*, Vol. 115, Sept. 23, 1946, p. 368.

manager and in that capacity had worked with labor leaders for the election of the national ticket.

The organization, then, entered the primary contest with the unit votes of most of the Republican counties and the six Legislative Districts of Baltimore city assured for Preston Lane. The problem posed was to devise a method of depriving Streett Baldwin of the County Unit vote of some of the southern counties. This problem was solved by injecting the very popular Millard Tawes from the Eastern Shore into the contest. Tawes was a widely respected conservative Democrat who had held the office of state comptroller without opposition in either the primaries or the general election for as long as most contemporaries could remember. Thereby, Baldwin's defeat was made certain and Lane's victory was virtually assured, because Tawes would take the conservative Eastern Shore vote away from Baldwin.

It should be understood that the desire on the part of most party leaders to defeat Streett Baldwin did not reflect any concern on their part for the sensibilities of the C.I.O. With the exception of Thomas D'Alesandro, the long-time New Dealing mayor of Baltimore city, and Jack Pollack, political leader of the lower socio-economic Fourth Legislative District, most of the party leaders shared Baldwin's views. However, the important fact to the Democratic organization was that Baldwin would have had virtually no chance of winning a general election. Therefore, Tawes was persuaded to enter the contest in order to deprive Representative Baldwin of the County Unit vote of the Eastern Shore counties. In all probability, Mr. Tawes did not enter the campaign with this object in view. However, it was the obvious effect of his candidacy.

The strategy was successful. Tawes carried every Eastern Shore county, Baldwin carried the Western Shore as expected, and Lane received the vote of the remaining counties, winning the nomination. Lane was subsequently elected governor by the narrowest of margins.

Economic and Social Divisions

Maryland's Democratic party is plagued with at least three fundamental divisions within the ranks of its partisans. First, there is a liberal-conservative schism, secondly, a religious difference, and thirdly, a racial issue. Baltimore city, one stronghold of the Democratic party, is a town composed in large part of laborers, immigrants, and Negroes. All three of these groups have become partisans of the New Deal brand of democracy. In addition to being inclined to vote for "liberal" candidates, they are also Catholic (over 50 per cent) and wet. The Eastern Shore white population, the other center of Democratic strength, is largely of Anglo-Saxon stock, unmixed with the new population that passed through Baltimore city on its way west. They are a conservative, rural, protestant people, whose opinions have their roots in the ante bellum South.

The 1934 and 1954 gubernatorial primaries and general elections, and the two Tydings contests of 1938 and 1950 illustrate the nature of the internal divisions that plague the Democratic party. An account of these ballot box battles will help make understandable the nature of the issues and incidents that divide the party.

In 1934, Governor Albert C. Ritchie was a candidate for his fifth nomination and election as governor of the state. He had been governor since 1919, winning election in four consecutive contests by comfortable majorities on a Democratic ticket which was in little favor elsewhere in the nation.

The reason for Governor Ritchie's political success until 1934 was his astute treading of the middle line of Maryland's political scene. In 1910, Ritchie, a native of Baltimore, was appointed "People's Counsel" to the Public Service Commission. According to the *Maryland Manual*, "It was in this capacity that Mr. Ritchie represented the people of Baltimore in his noteworthy fight for cheaper gas and electricity, which resulted in reducing the price of gas from 90 to 80 cents per 1000 cubic feet, and the price of electricity from 10 to 8½ cents per K.W.H."[1] Therefore, Ritchie was always assured of a substantial vote from Baltimore. In addition, he was a conservative States-Rights Democrat, who believed in economy and efficiency in government. This was a position that won for him the support of the influential Baltimore *Sun*, the business community in Baltimore city, and of Tidewater Maryland. When he extended his States-Rights position to include the prohibition amendment to the constitution he earned the support of the good German burghers of Baltimore city. And when he further extended the States-Rights principle to a refusal of President Harding's request that he dispatch state troopers to a strike scene in western Maryland,

---

[1] *Maryland Manual*, 1923, p. 193.

he elicited enthusiasm for his candidacy from even that rock-ribbed Republican community.

In 1934, however, Ritchie's ingeniously contrived coalition departed his camp both to the right and to the left. The conservative Eastern Shore left him because he was too liberal, and the liberals deserted him because of his conservatism. The good governor antagonized the Eastern Shore people in 1931 because of the investigations he initiated of a lynching that occurred in the area. Another reason for Ritchie's developing unpopularity among the Eastern Shore's God-fearing people was that his "wet" sympathies offended their moral sensibilities.

The "liberals" and laboring population of Baltimore city and western Maryland deserted the governor because in the flood-tide of the New Deal they felt it possible to elect a person considerably to the left of Mr. Ritchie. The governor had given evidence of a distinct coolness toward the Roosevelt New Deal, exhibiting extreme reluctance to take advantage of the "torrent" of money released by Washington. He defended his position on the basis of States-Rights. However, the magic of the States-Rights position had been rubbed away by depression, and the hungry could find little nourishment in the governor's fine-spun theories of government.

In the 1934 Democratic gubernatorial primary, Governor Ritchie was nominated, but his opponent in the primary, a political unknown, received a large vote from the Eastern Shore counties and Baltimore city. The size of the "protest vote" in the primary boded ill for the governor's chances in the general election. In the subsequent campaign, Nice, the Republican candidate, attacked Ritchie for his non-support of the New Deal. Mr. Nice's principal plank held that he would make a better New Dealer than Mr. Ritchie. The result was the election of a Republican governor in Maryland in a year that "yellow dogs" were being elected in Pennsylvania if only their names appeared under the Democratic label.

The locus of the defection from Ritchie's standard in 1934 as evidenced by the percentage-point change in the vote he received by counties from 1930-34 is quite interesting. The Baltimore *Sun* and the *New York Times* tended to ascribe Ritchie's loss in 1934 more to the lynching and liquor issues than the New Deal issue. According to this theory, it was the defection of the Eastern Shore people that defeated Ritchie and not the labor vote. The facts, however, indicate that the contrary was true, as Ritchie fared better on the Eastern Shore in the 1934 general election than in the 1930 election. Ritchie's good Eastern Shore showing was due to two factors: 1) the favorable reaction of the colored voters to the governor's stern actions in the 1931 lynching; and 2) the support which accrued to Ritchie from the Eastern Shore Bourbons because of Nice's espousal of the New Deal. However, outside the Eastern Shore section, the governor lost electoral ground in every county of the state, and particularly in Baltimore city, and western Maryland where there are many coal mines. Thus Ritchie's crop of votes failed during a Democratic rain, whereas he had prospered at the ballot box when the Republican sun had withered Democratic hopes throughout the land.

It is significant that the only two Republican governors elected by Maryland's voters since 1915 have been "liberals" (Nice and McKeldin). It has become a truism of Maryland politics that a Republican gubernatorial candidate, to be successful, must be more liberal than the Democratic candidate. The reason for this unorthodox state of affairs has its roots in the composition of the two parties. The center of Republican strength is in western Maryland. Because western Maryland is a coal and railroad center, a conservative Republican candidate loses strength in the section to a "liberal" Democrat. The centers of Democratic strength are in the Eastern Shore and Baltimore city. A conservative Republican when faced by a liberal Democrat can expect to gain strength in the Eastern Shore that will approximately compensate him for the strength lost in western Maryland. Consequently, Baltimore city's reaction to the candidates provides the key to the result, and, since 1932, the city has tended to support liberal Democratic candidates and to reject the more conservative candidates of that party.

The near-comic paradox of the two Tydings campaigns of 1938 and 1950 provides, perhaps, one of the more instructive lessons in the perils of Maryland politics. In the 1950 Democratic senatorial primary, one of Senator Tydings' opponents for the nomination, Robert Monaghan II, said of that sorely perplexed man: "The Tydings report [of the Armed Forces Committee investigating charges of communism in the State Department] has given the green light to Stalin's agents in this country to continue to gnaw at the foundations of our national security."[1] Colonel Mc-

---

[1] Baltimore *Sun*, September 1, 1950, p. 19.

Cormick of the *Chicago Tribune* also paid his respects to Senator Tydings. The Colonel, in his customarily mild manner, observed: "Senator Tydings is a supporter of the Iron Curtain and concentration camps for millions."[1]

Twelve years before the 1950 campaign, in 1938, Senator Tydings engaged in another contest for his Senate seat in which radicalism, communism and the C.I.O. were issues. In that campaign no less a personage than President Roosevelt pointed the finger of scorn at Senator Tydings as a man who had voted against the Agricultural Adjustment Act, the National Industrial Recovery Act, the Tennessee Valley Authority, the first Guffey coal bill, the National Labor Relations Act, the court plan, the reorganization bill and only "present" in the balloting on the Social Security Act.[2]

Few Republicans could boast so stern a record of unyielding opposition to New Deal measures. Tydings' reply to Roosevelt's barrage was two-fold. In the first place, he emphasized the "Free State" tradition of Marylanders; their unyielding opposition to outside interference in their affairs. In the second place, he accused his primary opponent, national Representative Davey Lewis, of communist proclivities. In speeches delivered in southern Maryland he tended to confuse the names of Davey Lewis and John L. Lewis. In fact, listeners were left with the distinct impression that his opponent was really John L., masquerading under the pseudonym of Davey.

---

[1] *Ibid.*, November 2, 1950, p. 19.
[2] See J. B. Shannon, "Presidential Politics in the South," *Journal of Politics*, Vol. 1, August, 1939, pp. 290-95.

The result of the 1938 primary was a resounding victory for Senator Tydings. He carried southern and central Maryland by lopsided margins, and four of Baltimore city's six Legislative Districts. The only counties he lost were in western Maryland, which were in Lewis' congressional district and which contain a large proportion of railroad and coal mine laboring people.

In 1950, the Senator was again successful in the primaries. However, in this primary, his opponents were unknowns without any organized support, and yet they polled a considerable vote in certain counties of the state. The counties in which the anti-Tydings vote was substantial (one-third or more) were, 1) St. Mary's, the Western Shore county with a population more than 70 per cent Catholic (1936 *Census of Religious Bodies*), and 2) the urban and suburban communities of Prince Georges and Baltimore counties, and Baltimore city.

The locus of the defection from the Tydings banner boded ill for Tydings' chances in the general election. The Senator had long since forfeited all claims to labor and Negro support in the cities, but had enjoyed overwhelming support in southern Maryland. However, the primary results indicated that the "communist" outcry had affected his popularity even in that area.

As though to compound the Senator's difficulties in the general election campaign, the Democratic gubernatorial primary of 1950 was also an unusually bitter contest. In that campaign, W. Preston Lane, the incumbent governor, was opposed by George Mahoney, a paving contractor of Baltimore city. Mr. Mahoney's

decision to contest the nomination was reportedly
motivated by his unceremonious dismissal by the
governor from his post as chairman of the State Racing
Commission.

The principal issue of the gubernatorial primary was
a 2 per cent sales tax, enacted during the Lane administration. The temper of the campaign can be judged
by a statement made by Mahoney. On September 3,
Mahoney said: "I am fighting against one of the most
powerful political machines that has ever ruled the
state. I am fighting that machine under every handi-
cap and barrier it can devise to hinder me. But I am
going to beat that machine and its powerful bosses
and become your governor, a free governor of the great
'Free State'."[1]

The day before the primary the Mahoney forces
published an advertisement in the *Sun* which attempted to summarize Mr. Mahoney's appeal to the voters.
It was a full page advertisement, which in appearance
smacked of the type of appeal made by used car
dealers to potential customers. Around the four sides
of the page were emblazoned the slogans: "MONEY
SAVED IS MONEY EARNED," "VOTE FOR MA-
HONEY AND SAVE," "MAHONEY IN ANNAPO-
LIS MEANS MORE MONEY IN YOUR POCK-
ETS," and in the center of the page, enclosed in great
boxes, were the promises "NO MORE SALES TAX,"
"SAVE MONEY WITH GEORGE MAHONEY,"
"SAVE 10 PERCENT ON YOUR INCOME TAX,"
"VETS BONUS."[2]

The results of the primary indicated that George

[1] Baltimore *Sun,* September 3, 1950, p. 40.
[2] Baltimore *Sun,* September 18, 1950, p. 17.

Mahoney had not misjudged his rational Maryland man. He emerged victorious in the popular vote by a narrow margin. However, because of Maryland's county unit system and because of Jack Pollack's zealous missionary efforts on behalf of Lane's candidacy in the city's Fourth Legislative District, Lane emerged the party's nominee. Mahoney carried the city by a substantial margin, 85,863 for Mahoney to 73,988 for Lane, but in the Fourth Legislative District the pattern of the city's vote was reversed and Lane was the winner by 11,137 to 9,641 votes for Mahoney, saving the nomination for Lane. Mahoney felt that he had been "robbed," but there was nothing he could do about the results of the primary. However, he was in a position to do something about the results of the general election.

In short, Senator Tydings and Governor Lane entered the general election campaign with three strikes or more against them: 1) many conservative and Catholic voters were alienated from the ticket by the communist issue; 2) the sales tax issue was a serious political liability throughout the state; 3) labor and the liberals could not generate enthusiasm for Senator Tydings, and Theodore McKeldin, the Republican gubernatorial candidate, appealed to this element; and 4) the party was badly split by the bitter gubernatorial primary. The result was overwhelming defeat for both Senator Tydings and Governor Lane in the general election. Senator Tydings lost strength in every county of the state, but particularly in the suburban and urban communities of Washington, D.C. and Baltimore city, areas where the communist issue seemed to have the greatest effect and where Theodore McKeldin made inroads on the liberal Democratic vote.

The 1954 gubernatorial primary was, in many respects, a repetition of the 1950 fiasco. Dr. H. C. (Curly) Byrd was the organization candidate in the Democratic primary. George Mahoney assumed, once again, the role of Jack the Giant Killer. Again, Mahoney tasted the sweet apple of victory only to have it turn into the sour grape of defeat, when again Jack Pollack's Fourth Legislative District in company with the Republican counties of western and southern Maryland, and the majority of the Eastern Shore counties turned the tide against the worthy paving contractor.

In the general election Dr. Byrd saw that he had little chance of wresting the Baltimore city vote from the confident hands of Governor Theodore McKeldin. Therefore, he sought to balance the expected city majority for McKeldin with a greater majority from southern Maryland. The device he employed was the time-honored race issue. The good University of Maryland President accused McKeldin of support for the school integration program. McKeldin's only reply was "shock" at the "unprincipled" tactics of his opponent.

Byrd is not a reactionary. His views on the race issue are probably not too dissimilar from those owned by Theodore McKeldin. Mr. Byrd was only trying to win an election. Byrd tried to be a liberal too. Among other things, former Senator Pepper was imported from Florida for a speech before a P.A.C. meeting, at which he wholeheartedly endorsed Dr. Byrd's candidacy. However, Dr. Byrd's efforts were to no avail. He improved the party's position in southern Maryland over the 1950 vote, but the loss of the colored vote in the cities at least balanced the gain. The extent of the colored voters' defection from the Democratic ranks may be measured by a comparison of the vote in two of Baltimore city's colored wards for the offices of governor and attorney general. In Ward 15 the vote for Democrat Byrd was 5,661 to 19,573 for McKeldin; and in the same ward, the Democratic candidate for the office of attorney general, Sodaro, received 12,898 votes to 6,925 votes for his Republican opponent. In Ward 27 the vote for governor was 15,993 for Byrd to 35,116 for McKeldin, and for attorney general the vote was 28,227 for the Democratic candidate to 18,103 for his Republican opponent. Therefore, in the 1954 primary the party attempted to retrieve its southern Maryland vote and succeeded to some extent, but in the process suffered the loss of a great deal of its Balimore city strength.

Conclusions

Prior to the New Deal period, Maryland and its Democratic party were dominated by a coalition of Tidewater Bourbons and Baltimore city political and business leaders. The coalition was inherently an uneasy marriage. The Tidewater Maryland side of the marriage bed was occupied by an Anglo-Saxon descendant of slaveowners who had inherited all their faults and virtues, whereas the other occupant was a winsome wench with German, Negro and Italian blood coursing through her veins. The alliance was pleasant so long as the maid did not venture to the window.

In 1933, Franklin Roosevelt's New Deal captured

the big city labor, immigrant and colored vote. Since
that time the relations between the urban and Tidewater Maryland Democratic political leaders have
been difficult. The present day grouping within Democratic ranks differs in numerous important respects
from the old. The most important difference is that
the new alliance, unlike the old which was between
business leaders and Bourbons, is between Bourbons
and Baltimore city politicians who must pay their respects to labor, the immigrant, and the Negro. Formerly, this vote could be bought with a drink or a
dollar bill. Today, legislation is demanded in payment.
This makes the new alliance more difficult to maintain.

The single cement that holds these two dissimilar
groups together is a common desire for the emoluments of public office. The constituents of both groups
of leaders vote Democratic. The Eastern Shore white
folk cast their votes for the party which, to them,
symbolizes the ideal of white supremacy. Many of
the Baltimore city voters place their "X" under the
Democratic standard because, to them, it is the party
of the common man. The important thing to the
political leaders, however, is the fact that both groups
vote Democratic.

The problem for the political leaders, then, is to
make the party image approximate the preconceptions
of the voters of both regions. The result is the production of candidates who sound liberal in the cities
and Bourbon in the country. These are Border State
politicians.

CHAPTER IX

MARYLAND TRENDS

In 1649, the Maryland Assembly passed the "Toleration Act," a milestone in the history of religious toleration. In 1856, Maryland cast the majority of its vote for Millard Fillmore, the Know-Nothing candidate for President, and ranked as the only state in the union to do so.

Maryland is replete with contradictions. The so-called "Fall Line" divides the state into two geographical and cultural halves. The Fall Line runs roughly from Washington to Baltimore, thence to Wilmington, Delaware. North and west of the Line, the land rises to form the Piedmont Plateau; south of the Line the topography flattens to become a part of the coastal plain, or Tidewater Maryland.

The early English settlers made their homes in southern or Tidewater Maryland. Rather extensive grants of land were made to the early settlers, and the type of crop grown was tobacco. Successful production of tobacco required large plantations and great numbers of unskilled labor. The first requirement was supplied by the King and Lord Baltimore, and the second by the importation of slaves.

The year of the first United States Census, 1790, there were 191,627 white residents of Maryland and 103,036 slaves. The vast majority of the slaves were in the southern portion of the state, leaving the southern section's population very nearly evenly divided in number between slaves and non-slaves. For example, in Charles county there were, in 1790, 10,124 white residents and 10,985 slaves; in Prince Georges county, 10,004 whites and 11,176 slaves; in Anne Arundel, 11,664 whites and 10,103 slaves. These statistics indicate the extent to which a plantation system flourished at an early date in southern Maryland's history.

Until about 1732 the southern half of Maryland was the only section in which there had been any considerable settlement. Therefore, at that date the state was clearly married to the South. Great Georgian mansions were erected and the Cavalier mores and customs were the culture of the region. The white population in these southern counties, according to the 1790 census, was, in most counties, 90 per cent or more of English and Welsh extraction. In the state as a whole, more than 80 per cent of the white population was of the same extraction.

An important feature of the settlement of the southern counties was the colonization of the St. Mary's county area by Catholics escaping religious persecution in England. This area remains dominantly Catholic. According to the 1936 *Census of Religious Bodies*, 73 per cent of the population in St. Mary's county and 37 per cent of the Charles county population were Catholic. Nineteen per cent of Maryland's population were of the Catholic faith in 1936.

After 1732, the cultural and political profile of Maryland underwent a transformation. Between 1732 and 1790 Maryland changed from a southern state into a middle or border state. The occasion for this change was the settlement of the state's western counties. Many of the people who entered this frontier came from Pennsylvania and were of German extraction. According to the 1790 census, 4,356, or approximately 30 per cent of Washington county's population, were of German extraction; and in Frederick county 5,137 of the 26,937 residents were German (Allegany and Garrett county had not been formed at this date). The 9,493 Germans living in the two counties represented 84 per cent of the total German population in the state. Later influxes of German population tended to move into this same area and into Baltimore city.

The new population's culture was as distant from the old Tidewater Maryland culture as is the Nama Hottentot's steatopygia from Dior's "H" line. The new settlers preferred small farms to plantations, barns to mansions, wheat to tobacco. Further, they abhorred slavery. Much of the nation's abolitionist propaganda and sentiment stemmed from the Germanic element in Maryland's and the nation's population. Before the Civil War, these Germanic people tended to be Democrats in a Whig state, abolitionists in a slave stronghold, a cohesive ethnic group in a nativist community. After the Civil War, many of the Germans became Republicans in a Democratic state.

The close of the Civil War also witnessed the transfer of the allegiance of the slave-owning aristocrats of southern Maryland from the Whigs to the Democratic faith. However, instead of adopting the tenets of Jefferson, the former slave-holders remoulded the state's Democratic party into a reflection of their own philosophy of government. Therefore, after the Civil War, the Democratic party in Maryland was Democratic in name only. It was the old Whig party with a new name. One indication of this development was the name used by the Bourbons during the transition period from Whig to Democrat to designate their political faith. The party name used by the Bourbons was "conservative" as opposed to the Republican or Union party.

People both within and without the state of Maryland generally refer to it as a "Democratic" state. This is true in only a very special sense. Three out of five of the state's registered voters call themselves Democrats. Officials wearing the Democratic label control most of the offices at the county level, and the state's General Assembly has been dominated by so-called Democrats in virtually every session since 1871. In spite of these statistics, however, it would be a rash person, indeed, who would describe Maryland as a "dominantly" Democratic state.

Four salient facts demonstrate the marginal nature of Maryland's vote, with respect to its division between the two major parties; 1) in presidential elections from 1896 to 1956 the state has voted more often Republican than Democratic (in 10 of 16 elections); 2) in gubernatorial elections the state has most often voted Democratic, voting Republican in only five gubernatorial contests since 1871, two of these occurring in 1950 and 1954; 3) the state outside Baltimore city has, historically, been extraordinarily evenly divided between the two parties in both the gubernatorial and presidential contests (the Republican party has received the larger vote outside Baltimore city in 9 of 22 gubernatorial and 10 of 21 presidential contests since 1871); 4) the vote of Baltimore city more often than not determines the victor in presidential and gubernatorial elections.

From 1895 to 1932, the tendency of Baltimore city

was to cast a majority of its vote for Democratic gubernatorial candidates and Republican presidential aspirants. Since 1932, however, the situation in Baltimore city has been reversed. Instead of being a stronghold for Democratic gubernatorial candidates it has become an even greater source of votes for the party's presidential aspirants. The reason for Baltimore city's tendency to support Republican presidential candidates from 1896 through 1928, and Democratic gubernatorial candidates over the same period is compounded of business attitudes toward the free silver party after 1896, the attitude of the German population toward the national Democratic party after the Civil War and World War I, and the susceptibility of the colored and immigrant vote to manipulation. The basic reason, though, is probably to be found in the attitude of the business community toward the party of economic nostrums after its nomination of William Jennings Bryan in 1896. The question might logically be posed, then, why didn't these leaders travel the full route and support Republican candidates in the state as well as nationally? The answer is that the realities of the power structure in Maryland militated against alliance with the Republican party. This is true because the system whereby seats are apportioned in Maryland's General Assembly makes Republican control of the General Assembly an almost impossible task.

According to Maryland's constitution, each county and legislative district is entitled to one senator. Representation in the House of Delegates is adjusted according to population, with the least populous counties getting two delegates and the most populous counties and legislative districts receiving a maximum representation of six delegates.[1] This system of apportionment results in a gross under-representation of the relatively populous Republican counties of western Maryland, and of Baltimore city; and over-representation of the thinly populated Democratic counties of the Eastern Shore. Therefore, in the election of state officials the business and financial community found it expedient to support Democratic candidates. They did so by furnishing the money to the political leaders by means of which the laboring, colored, and immigrant voters were persuaded either not to vote or to vote conservative Democratic in gubernatorial elections.

Following 1932, a fundamental political revolution occurred in Maryland. Due to New Deal measures relative to labor and the Negro, the labor, immigrant, and colored vote was, to a great extent, snatched from the hands of the business and Bourbon communities. In Baltimore city, after 1932, it was no longer possible to deliver votes for conservative Republican candidates nationally, and for conservative Democrats locally. On the contrary, the Baltimore city vote tended thereafter to support liberal candidates nationally and to reject conservative Democrats locally.

---

[1] The Constitution provides:
    a. That each county and the six Legislative Districts shall be entitled to one Senator.
    b. Membership in the House of Delegates is apportioned to the counties and six Legislative Districts as follows:

less than 18,000 population	— 2 delegates
18,000 - 28,000	— 3 delegates
28,000 - 40,000	— 4 delegates
40,000 - 55,000	— 5 delegates
55,000 and over	— 6 delegates

    c. By a 1950 constitutional amendment the membership of the House of Delegates was frozen at its present number.

This development has tended to place the state's power structure in disequilibrium. Eastern Shore Bourbon candidates for state office need the vote of Baltimore city in the general elections. It is possible for Tidewater Maryland to nominate a candidate for high office through the county unit system without the support of Baltimore city, but it is impossible for them to elect him once nominated. On the other hand, a candidate too closely identified with the New Deal forfeits the support of Tidewater Maryland in a primary. Therefore, the basic dilemma of Maryland's Democratic party is whether it is a liberal big city party serving the interests of labor, the Negro and ethnic groups; or a conservative Southern party catering to white southern Maryland and the financial and business community. Obviously, a single party cannot do both. However, Maryland's Democratic leaders have exerted heroic efforts in just that direction.

Democratic candidates in the Eastern Shore section of Tidewater Maryland warn of the dangers to white hegemony in Republican rule. Democratic candidates in Baltimore city's Fourth Legislative District point with pride to Franklin Roosevelt's efforts in behalf of the Negro and warn of the dangers to Negro progress implicit in Republican rule.

Political Change

Figure 24 identifies the locale of the political change that has occurred in the presidential elections, 1916–1952. Analysis of the figure leads to the conclusion that the most marked political change experienced in the state in recent years has been a result of four developments: 1) the creation under the aegis of the

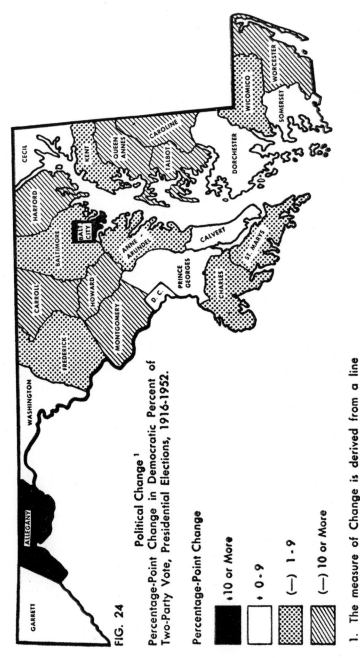

FIG. 24

Political Change [1]

Percentage-Point Change in Democratic Percent of
Two-Party Vote, Presidential Elections, 1916-1952.

Percentage-Point Change

- ◆ 10 or More
- ◆ 0 - 9
- (—) 1 - 9
- (—) 10 or More

1. The measure of Change is derived from a line
of regression or secular trend line computed for each
county.

New Deal of a labor or liberal political grouping which has wrested Baltimore city's labor, immigrant and colored vote from the conservative elements that once dominated it; 2) the mining-camp type population movement of suburbanites from Washington, D. C. and Baltimore city into surrounding counties; 3) the movement of the colored population from southern Maryland into the cities; and 4) the reaction of Tidewater Maryland to the New Deal.

Figure 24 shows that the plus Republican change that has occurred in Maryland over the period 1916-1952 has been considerable and widespread. This change is concentrated in two areas; mainly, the counties bordering Baltimore city and Washington, D. C.; and the Eastern Shore counties.

Population change explains the plus Republican change that has occurred in the counties adjacent to Washington, D. C. and Baltimore city. These counties were largely rural farm communities at the turn of the century and were Democratic strongholds, but they have since become centers of a swelling suburban population. Proportionately, Maryland's suburban population is probably the largest in the nation. Prince Georges and Montgomery counties, bordering Washington, D. C., have grown from populations of 20,898 and 30,451 in 1900 to 194,182 and 164,401, respectively, in 1950. Most of this population increase has been a product of the movement outward from Washington, D. C. of the better paid business and professional class into the Maryland countryside. Similarly, the population of Baltimore county has increased from 90,755 in 1900 to 270,273 in 1950, most of which has come from Baltimore city. The total potential vote of these three suburban counties is 394,347 or 26 per cent of the total potential vote of the state (1950).

Therefore, the plus Republican trend evident in the suburban counties, save Prince Georges which has remained relatively unchanged,[1] has had an important impact on the political balance of the state. One of the most important effects has been the increased Republican vote from these counties in gubernatorial elections. The suburban people are Republican in both state and national politics. They are foreign to the old power structure of the state. Furthermore, it is difficult to integrate them into it because most of the colored population which was formerly resident in these counties has departed in search of a less rarified atmosphere. Therefore, it is difficult to instill in the hearts of the suburban folk a compelling concern for "white supremacy," and thus a fear of "black Republican" rule.

The Eastern Shore is the other section of the state in which a pronounced plus Republican trend is evident. The plus Republican political change in the Eastern Shore area is composed of two contradictory parts. In the first place, the Bourbons of the area dislike the New Deal and all its works. They blame it for the new power structure of the state. The most used political hate word in the section is the C.I.O.-P.A.C. This adjective will elicit almost as much

---

[1] The decline in the percentage of Prince Georges county that is colored, from 43 per cent in 1900 to 12 per cent in 1950, probably accounts, in part, for the slight plus Democratic trend in that county, despite the influx of a suburban population from Washington, D. C. In addition, Prince Georges suburban population is at a lower economic level than that of Montgomery. According to the 1950 census, 53.3 per cent of Montgomery's families had an income in excess of $5,000, compared to a figure of 35.8 per cent for Prince Georges county.

emotion from the white residents of the area as the term "carpetbagger." Therefore, the "Bourbons" or rulers of the area are currently most unenthusiastic about the national Democratic party, which they tend to identify with the C.I.O.-P.A.C.

The changed political and geographic position of the colored voter is another important ingredient in political change throughout the state, including the Eastern Shore. There has been a great exodus of Negroes from Tidewater Maryland to the cities. In the cities it is more difficult to intimidate the colored voter. Therefore, he enjoys proportionately greater freedom in the exercise of the franchise, and this vote is no longer controlled by conservative interests.

Even in Tidewater Maryland, however, the colored person is voting with greater freedom. This fact is reflected in two contrary trends in the Tidewater section. Those counties with a large colored population, which are traditionally Republican, and where the Negro has traditionally voted freely, have tended to increase their percentage Democratic vote. Calvert, Dorchester and Somerset counties, all Tidewater Republican counties, show a plus Democratic trend over the period 1916-1952. On the other hand, the Democratic Tidewater counties with a considerable colored population have registered a plus Republican trend. This is partially due to the fact that the rural Negro is still largely though decreasingly Republican, and now that he votes with greater freedom in the Democratic counties, the result is a plus Republican trend.

As a consequence of the changing position of the Negro in Maryland politics, it is no longer politically profitable to brandish the "white supremacy" bogey.

Dr. Byrd discovered this fact in the 1954 gubernatorial election. His identification with the white supremacy issue cost him many votes in Baltimore city, and did not appreciably improve his position in southern Maryland.

As has already been indicated, the plus Democratic change which has occurred in Baltimore city in presidential elections represents a political revolution of more than ordinary proportions. Instead of manufacturing majorities for conservative Democrats in state elections and for conservative Republicans in national elections the city registers large pluralities for New Dealers and helps defeat conservative Democratic candidates for governor.

The reasons for this change are many. However, fundamentally it is a result of the organization of the forces of labor and the new-found political awareness of the Negro. It is impossible for a Jack Pollack in his Fifteenth Ward to produce a majority for a conservative Democratic candidate, even if he were so inclined. For example, when Pollack distributed his Fourth District "slate" in the general election of 1954, the name of Dr. Byrd, the white supremacy Democratic candidate for governor, was not included.

The counties of Garrett, Allegany, and Washington in western Maryland are the only counties outside Baltimore city that react favorably when the New Deal is at issue. All three counties show a plus Democratic change over the period 1916-1952. A comparison of the 1946 and 1948 congressional elections demonstrates the New Deal bias of these counties. In the 1946 campaign for national representative in Maryland's 6th Congressional District the New Deal was

not at issue. In that election the three western counties cast a "normal" Republican vote. In the 1948
campaign, however, the Democratic candidate in the
District was a New Deal advocate, whereas his Republican opponent condemned it and all its works.
Comparison of the 1946 and 1948 election returns
shows that the counties of Garrett, Allegany, and
Washington reacted positively to the New Deal issue
by casting a greatly increased percentage Democratic
vote. The favorable response of the three counties to
the New Deal issue is attributable to their compara-
tively large laboring population (mining and railroad).

The Baltimore *Sun* has also been an important element in the political change experienced by the state.
The *Sun* is a conservative force and is Maryland's
only state-wide newspaper. The paper has been a
consistent spokesman for the "old" Bourbon order. A
governor like Albert Ritchie and a president such as
Grover Cleveland represent the best of all possible
worlds to the *Sun*. Needless to say, the *Sun* has been
displeased with the Democratic party for lo' these
many years.

Conclusions

There have been three important developments in
Maryland's political scene in recent years: 1) the phe-
nomenal increase in the state's suburban population
caused by the outward movement from the cities of
Washington and Baltimore; 2) the new political position of the Negro; and 3) the change in the state's
power structure wrought by the New Deal, a change
which is most noticeably reflected in the vote of Baltimore city. The net effect of all three of these develop-

ments has been to reduce the "normal" percentage Democratic vote in the state.

It is a fiction to refer to Maryland as dominantly Democratic. It is Democratic only because of the method of apportioning state representatives and senators. In all probability, the majority of the state's voters as of today are Republican by inclination or tradition.

This is true because of the Republican proclivities of the suburban populace; because of the traditionally Republican tendencies of the state's large rural colored population; and because of the schism in the Democratic party between its liberal or labor element and its Bourbon group.

The difficulties of the Democratic party are compounded by the conservative Baltimore *Sun*. This paper, which enjoys a wide circulation in southern Maryland, tends to encourage these people in their inclination to assign the role of "devil" to the C.I.O.-P.A.C., and, in turn, to associate this "devil" with the national Democratic party.

CHAPTER X
THE UNIFYING THEME

IN VERY GENERAL TERMS, the unifying theme found in the political structure of the Border States consists of four parts. First, the unique settlement pattern of the Border States and the differential reaction of elements of the population to events such as the Civil War has been primarily responsible for the evolution of a three-party political pattern. Secondly, the three-party political pattern has produced within the dominant or Democratic party a distinctive type of political organization which is designed to bridge the gap between the warring factions of the Democratic party and thus enable the party to win elections. Thirdly, in order to win elections both parties find it necessary to offer candidates who can capture the urban vote, because of the rigidly narrow total political division in all the Border States outside the urban sections. Fourthly, the settlement pattern, the differential reaction of elements of the population to policies of the political parties, and factionalism represent primary causative agents of the type of political change observed in the Border States.

Figure 25 demonstrates the essential similarity of the Border States in terms of both the division between the two major parties and long-run trends. As the figure indicates, all of the Border States were predominantly Democratic in presidential elections in 1872, but it also shows that the Republican party steadily gained strength in every Border State until 1932. In 1932, the Border States once again became

Democratic strongholds, but the long-run plus Republican trend again became evident after that date. It is because of the fact that the Democratic party still rules in all four Border States that it has been necessary to concentrate upon Democratic intra-party politics in order to tell the story of Border State politics; for it has been within the Democratic party that the important decisions concerning "who shall rule" have been made. However, the Republican party is inexorably gaining ground in the Border States. In all probability, future studies of *Politics in the Border States* will be increasingly concerned with the Republican party.

As the Border States become less and less like the South, politically and culturally, and more and more like the Middle West, the South becomes increasingly akin to the Border States of yesteryear. There is good reason to believe that the Border States represent a political and cultural model that the South is destined to copy. Industrialization and urbanization in the South are producing a mixed culture, and the political impact of these culture changes are being reflected in the political behavior of the South, as witness the 1952 and 1956 presidential elections. Thus an understanding of Border State politics of today and yesterday should provide insight into the South of tomorrow.

We turn now to a discussion of the unifying theme found in political developments in the Border States. It is a theme which is helping to integrate the Border States into the nation today, and which should have the same effect upon the South tomorrow.

FIGURE 25

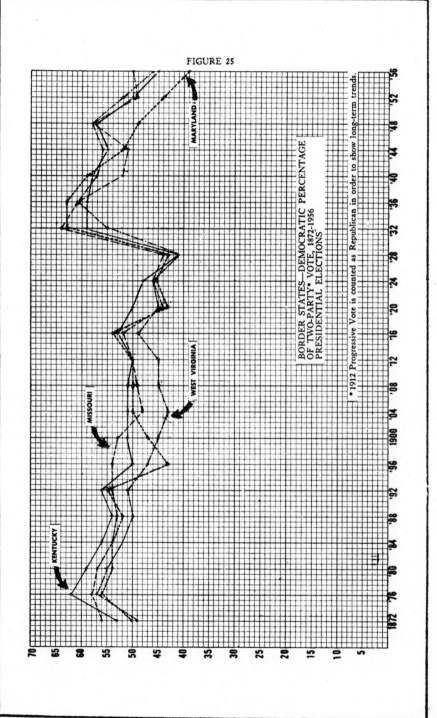

BORDER STATES—DEMOCRATIC PERCENTAGE
OF TWO-PARTY* VOTE, 1872-1956
PRESIDENTIAL ELECTIONS

* 1912 Progressive Vote is counted as Republican in order to show long-term trends.

The Border State Settlement Pattern

The Border States have in common a unique population development. Each state was settled at an early date by slaveholders who introduced a plantation-type economy and culture. In Missouri, the area settled by slaveholders is known as Little Dixie; in Kentucky as the Bluegrass; in West Virginia as the Greenbrier Plateau; and in Maryland as the Tidewater region. The Bourbons were largely Whig partisans prior to the Civil War and were dominantly Democratic thereafter.

The mountains of all four Border States were also settled at an early date. The people who made their homes in the Missouri Ozarks were the sons and daughters of the folk who built their cabins in the hills of Kentucky, Tennessee, and Virginia. In most instances, the hill people of the Border States have been aligned with the Republican party since the Civil War.

The rural areas outside the mountains and slave-holding areas were initially settled by yeoman farmers from the Upper South. Many of these people owned one or two slaves, but few were great slaveowners in the tradition of Margaret Mitchell. The people living in these areas of the Border States tended to ally themselves with the Jacksonian Democratic party prior to the Civil War, and remained Democratic thereafter.

Therefore, the principal change in the Border State alignment resulting from the Civil War was the transformation of the slaveowners into Democrats, and the making of Republicans of the freed slaves. As a result, the Border States became Democratic strongholds, but within a two-party framework.

Following the Civil War, the source of the Border States' new population tended to change. Instead of originating largely from the Upper South, as was the case prior to 1860, an increasing proportion of the new population entered the states from the North, and, therefore, was largely Republican in terms of its political tendencies. In addition, an increasing number of Republican-inclined Germans entered the states after the Civil War.

A more important development, however, was the population growth of the coal producing areas and the cities. The politically significant aspect of the new population in the cities and coal areas was its susceptibility to political manipulation. Initially, the existence of a manipulable urban and coal vote operated to the advantage of the business community, making possible the defeat of "liberal" candidates.

Franklin Roosevelt and his New Deal, however, transferred effective control of a sizeable proportion of the urban and coal vote from the hands of the business community to those of organized labor. Therefore, because labor has tended to support Democratic candidates since 1932, the Democratic party in the Border States has become the party of a cook's mixture of Bourbons, yeoman farmers, and laboring people. The Democratic party received a large vote from the urban working class districts before 1932, but the vote was not issue oriented. The important thing about the vote created by the New Deal is its essentially "labor" character; a vote cast for liberal Democrats, but not for Bourbon nominees.

Three-Party States

One of the principal theses of this study of *Politics in the Border States* has been the three-party character of the Border State political scene. The near-universal stereotype of the American political scene is of two great parties which periodically contest control of governments at the local, state, and national levels. In the Border States, at least, this stereotype falls short of accurately representing the true nature of the party system.

In the Border States there exist concentrations of Republican and Democratic strength in certain well defined social and economic sections of the states. In these areas few contests take place for offices at the local level. However, when the combined votes of these centers of Democratic and Republican strength are joined, the result is a rigidly narrow numerical division between the two major parties. Therefore, at the state level a contest takes place for control of the major offices.

Since the Civil War, the Democratic party has usually won the state-wide elections and thus has been the dominant party in the Border States (the single exception being West Virginia where the Republican party was dominant from 1896 and until 1932). Therefore, the struggles for control of that party have been decisive in determining "Who shall rule?" However, the Republican party has always been large enough to threaten Democratic hopes when Democratic factionalism has erupted. The nature of Democratic factionalism flows directly from the previous discussion of the composition of the party as determined by population movements and the reactions of certain elements of the population to events and political policies of the two major parties.

In general, there are two Democratic parties in the Border States. One Democratic party is the party of the Bourbons. This Democratic party is the political vehicle of the gentry, protecting the community from such "evils" as labor unions and "black and tan" rule. It is the party to which a "gentleman" belongs, because only colored people and "hillbillies" belong to the Republican party. The other Democratic party is the refuge of the "Common Man." It is to this political party that the urban Negroes, coal miners, urban workers, and yeoman farmers belong. On general election day both of these Democratic parties are asked to vote for a single candidate.

The intra-party conflicts of the Democratic party correspond more closely to the stereotype of the two-party system than do the interparty general election battles between Democratic and Republican forces. The first is often a conflict between the yeoman farmers and the laborers on the one hand and the Bourbons on the other. The second, or general election battles, is commonly a war for control of patronage and contracts rather than a conflict of interests.

The Republican party has, historically, been a conservative or "stand pat" party in the Border States. The Republican party is conservative because of its composition. It does not contain the contradictory elements found in Democratic ranks. The mountain people who have long provided the Republican party with a large proportion of its votes are conservative in the tradition of the isolated person. The other important groups in the party have been the Negro and urban business leaders. The Negro, until recently, has represented a manipulable vote and therefore provided a political bulwark for the business community against "liberal" candidates.

The Rooseveltian New Deal introduced many important changes into the Border State political arena. Prior to the New Deal, the vote of such areas as the West Virginia and Kentucky mining sections and the urban centers could be used to defeat "liberal" candidates in the Democratic primaries, and, failing that, in the general elections. Since the New Deal much of this vote has been lost by the Bourbons to labor leaders. Therefore, Democratic party factionalism has become increasingly intense as the policy divisions within the party have widened.

Political Organization

It is in the realm of political organization that a partial solution to the seemingly insoluble problem of Democratic factionalism has been found. In two of the Border States (Kentucky and West Virginia) in which Democratic factionalism has been particularly pronounced, strong "organizational" groups have evolved. In Kentucky, the "organization" is called the Administration faction; in West Virginia, the Neely-Hanna group.

The common denominator of these Democratic organizations is the fact that they provide a bridge between the social and economic factions of the party. The political leaders of both Bourbon and "liberal" Democratic areas own in common a desire to retain the emoluments of power. Each recognizes that factionalism is likely to deprive them of these emoluments. Therefore, they acknowledge the value of a strong central organization which is capable of asserting its authority independent of the social and economic divisions of the party.

The strength of the "organizations" rests in the governor's patronage and the large primary vote which they can register from the Republican and low income areas of their states through the use of this patronage. With this vote base, the organization negotiates alliances with the social and economic segments of the party from a position of strength. The objective of the organization is to select candidates and to pursue policies which will not antagonize any important segment of the party because, even though primary victory may be obtained while ignoring one segment of the party, the result of such tactics is often defeat in the general election.

In Missouri and Maryland state politics revolves, to a very considerable extent, around powerful city machines rather than around a state-wide "organization" dominated by the governor. The power of the city organizations in these two states stems from their ability to swing large blocs of votes behind candidates. The significance of the New Deal was that it transferred control over (or at least introduced competition for) the manipulable city vote from conservative to liberal or labor groups. The function of the city organization is similar to that of the state organizations in Kentucky and West Virginia. It provides a bridge between the various elements within the Democratic party by attempting to nominate candidates who will not be anathema to any group within the party and who can win in the general election.

The choice in the Border States, insofar as political organization is concerned, seems to be between a powerful state machine with a strong governor or a weak governor and political domination by the city machines.

The Border State Candidates

In all the Border States the total division between the Republican and Democratic parties has been exceedingly narrow and rigid in the tradition-bound rural areas. The rootless urban vote, on the other hand, has been subject to mercurial change from election to election. Therefore, the vote cast by urban areas has often been a crucial factor in determining the winner of Border State elections.

Prior to 1932 the urban vote was, in the main, controlled by conservative elements. Therefore, the successful candidates for office tended to be conservative. Since 1932, however, and the Roosevelt revolution which transferred effective control over much of the manipulable urban vote from the business community to labor organizations, the urban vote has been inclined toward "liberal" candidates.

The net result has been that even though the composition or at least the leadership of both parties is probably largely conservative, the realities of the political situation tend to force both parties to nominate relatively "liberal" candidates for office.

Political Change

The settlement pattern of the Border States, combined with events which have had a differential impact on elements of the population; factionalism; and political organization are the principal factors responsible for the type of political change that has occurred in the Border States.

The entrance of new people with a different cultural background in any significant numbers into a state is virtually certain to work changes on the political character of the community. This has been the experience of the Border States; and in most instances the population change has worked to the advantage of the Republican party. As has already been noted, an increasing proportion of the new population entering the Border States since the Civil War has been from the north, and, therefore, Republican-inclined. In addition, the changing composition of the Border States' political parties has helped intensify intraparty strife within the Democratic party. In turn, the intraparty strife has cost the Democratic party many adherents. For example, in West Virginia and Maryland, the Bourbon elements of the party have tended to desert the Democratic party because of their feeling that the party is dominated by organized labor.

The Republican party has suffered less from factional strife than has the Democratic party. This has been due to the absence of policy conflicts between the conservative mountain adherents of the party and the equally conservative urban elements of the Republican party. The single intraparty conflict which has cost the Republican party any considerable number of votes involved the colored element in the party. Prior to 1932, Republican leaders looked upon the colored vote as a "captive" vote. The colored people literally had "no place to go" other than the Republican camp. The Democratic party, prior to 1932, did little to encourage the colored people to think that they'd be welcomed as Democratic voters.

Therefore, the Republican leaders tended to neglect their colored friends in terms of patronage and the other emoluments of power. Consequently, an only half-articulated resentment developed among colored political leaders against their erstwhile friends and protectors, the Republican office holders. In the thirties, when Franklin D. Roosevelt offered colored leaders political recognition in exchange for votes, the dam of colored resentment burst and the Republican party lost a considerable proportion of its colored supporters.

The most decided political change to occur in recent years was the percentage-point increase in Democratic vote in the coal sections of the Border States after 1932. The increase in Democratic vote among the coal miners was not, fundamentally, a depression phenomenon. Neither did it represent a mere expression of gratitude on the part of the miners for social and economic reforms, although this was present. Basically, the increase in Democratic vote in the coal sections was due to the overturn in the power structure worked by unionization. Prior to the New Deal, the coal operators "voted" their workmen with relative impunity. Since 1932, the miners have tended to listen more closely to their union leaders' suggestions relative to their voting behavior than to the operators. Similar, though less spectacular changes, occurred in urban areas with large laboring populations.

A significant aspect of political change as it has occurred in the Border States is its relationship to political organization. In the absence of profound population change or the impact of divisive issues, strongly Democratic communities tend to become more Democratic, and strongly Republican areas more Republican. This tendency has been particularly marked in the low income, traditionally Republican communities of the Border States. Outside the urban and coal communities, the strongly Republican areas of the Border states have shown an almost universal trend in a plus Republican direction.

The poverty of these areas is an important element in the plus Republican change which has occurred; poverty which the New Deal did little to relieve. However, political organization is another variable of considerable importance in explaining the political change in the low income mountain counties. In most of the mountain counties strong Republican organizations dominate the politics of the community. A person living in a community which is dominated by a single political group must learn to live with the political authorities or suffer many unpleasant consequences. The "unpleasant" consequences include such items as social ostracism; high tax assessments; inability to obtain contracts for the delivery of goods and services to political entities; and difficulty in obtaining services from the county or city governments, such as the repair of roads, removal of ice and snow. Therefore, the citizen in such communities usually finds it expedient to conform to the dominant political ideology.

No effort has been made in these pages to present any thesis of economic determinism insofar as political change is concerned. However, as elsewhere, the economies of the various regions of the Border States have played a central role in determining the political predilections of their inhabitants. In the Border States the results have been somewhat surprising. As has been noted, the least wealthy rural sections of the Border States tend to be Republican-oriented, whereas the wealthier rural sections tend to be Democratic strongholds. The explanation for this phenomenon, of course, goes back to the Civil War and the contrasting reactions of the slaveholders and the mountain people to the policies of the two parties during that conflict.

Since the Civil War, the less well-to-do rural sections have, if anything, become more firmly attached to the Republican party. In addition to population change, political organization, and the fact that these people were not greatly helped by the New Deal (they are still poor), another important factor responsible for plus Republican change in the poor counties is the monolithic power structure in such communities. In the low income counties, no organized force exists which can challenge the influence of the anti-New Deal business community. Therefore, the reaction of the business community to the New Deal has been transmitted to the community without the modifying impact of the point of view of other organized groups. The Republican party has, of course, benefited from this situation. In the Bourbon counties the ruling elements have become increasingly disenchanted with the policies of the national Democratic party. The result has been a continuing plus Republican change in most Border State Bourbon counties, and particularly in the rural Bourbon areas.

The Border State industrial centers have not shown a consistent pattern of political behavior. Since 1932, such cities as St. Louis and Baltimore, and the coal mining sections of West Virginia and Kentucky have become strongholds for the New Deal brand of Democracy. On the other hand, the New Deal gains of the Democratic party have evaporated in such cities as Louisville, Kentucky and Charleston, West Virginia. The explanation for this anomalous political behavior in urban areas seems to rest in the character of the industries which are located in these cities. Where the industries are small and diversified, such as in Louisville, or where the laboring population is largely non-union oriented, such as in Charleston's chemical industry, the result is a plus Republican trend since 1932. However, where large industrial unions are dominant, such as in the coal and steel industries, the 1932 gains of the Democratic party have been sustained and in some places augmented. Thus where labor has been successful in organizing industry the Roosevelt revolution has been made permanent. Where widespread labor organization has not taken place, the Democratic gains of the New Deal period have dissipated or disappeared.

Therefore, Democratic gains in the Border States have tended to appear in areas with large colored populations and where organized labor is strong, i.e., in the coal and highly urbanized areas. On the other hand, Republican gains have tended to be concentrated in sections which have received large influxes of new population from the north and in low income rural areas. In Maryland, where the new population is predominantly suburbanite, the cause of plus Republican change is identical to that of areas receiving a northern population, i.e., the Republican bias of the new population.

Some Generalizations

As many observers have noted, basically a political party exists as a means of getting enough votes to win elections. And, as Herring puts it, in order to get enough votes to win an election the party must be an "alliance of interests."

The dominant "alliance of interests" in the Border States consists of 1) the Democratic organization; 2) the Bourbons or conservative Democrats; and 3) the "liberal" New Deal and Jacksonian Democrats. It is instructive to re-examine the political process by which this alliance manages to maintain political power in the Border States.

The Democratic "organization," as such, is a distinct entity because it controls a body of votes in Democratic primaries which is relatively independent of the social and economic groupings of the party. This vote is derived primarily from the rural low income counties of the state, and particularly the low income Republican counties. The reason for organization control of the low income counties in primaries is the relative importance of patronage and contracts to the Democratic organization in these sections.

The "organization" has one consuming interest, the winning of elections. Ideological considerations as such are of only limited importance to the organization. Therefore the efforts of organization people are directed toward securing as many votes as possible for Democratic candidates in the general election and to winning primary contests. It is because of this fact that the organization acts as a bridge between the

Bourbon or conservative Democrats and their more liberal brethren.

The organization may and usually does ally itself with a particular economic group in the party in order to secure victory in the primary; for example, the United Mine Workers in West Virginia is commonly allied with the Statehouse group in Democratic primaries. However, the organization must always remember that victory in the primary is never conclusive, as the Republican party always poses an electoral threat in the general election. Therefore, the organization must do its best to avoid irredeemable factional cleavages within Democratic ranks. It attempts to accomplish this objective by proposing candidates for nomination to state-wide office who are not overly repugnant to any faction of the party, and by the support of policies acceptable to all factions of the party. Thus the Statehouse group, although always friendly to labor's claims in West Virginia, engineered the defeat of the United Mine Worker-backed Fire Boss bill and thereby retrieved much support from the Bourbon faction of the party. It was this maneuver which enabled the Statehouse faction to achieve victory in the 1952 Democratic gubernatorial primary in West Virginia.

It is significant that Missouri, the Border State in which Democratic factionalism is least intense, has the weakest political organization among the states studied. There would seem to be a relationship between the degree of political organization and the intensity of factionalism. As has been noted, the single chain that binds Bourbon and liberal Democrats together is a common desire for the spoils of office.

Therefore, where factionalism imperils political victory, the political leaders of all factions are often willing to submit to a strong executive and, therefore, a strong central political organization in the interest of party victory.

Interest group leaders, unlike the political leaders, aren't very concerned about the results of elections as such. Most interest group leaders share the sentiment voiced by Milton Smith, President of the Louisville and Nashville Railroad, when he said, "Damn the Democrats. Damn the Republicans. It is nothing but a dirty scramble to see who shall hold the offices—we are not office holders, we are not office seekers." Milton Smith also detailed those items he did seek from the political leaders. He told the Democratic leaders of Kentucky at the turn of the century to "Shut them off—don't let them abuse the corporations." By "them" Mr. Smith referred to important Democratic leaders who sought legislation regulating the railroads and who wished to impose additional taxes on them. Thus the objective of any interest group, be it labor, business, farm, church, or reform, is to obtain and maintain a political atmosphere in which their enterprises will prosper.

The political power of particular categories of interest groups is a subject that often puzzles the student of politics. Political pundits sometimes wax maudlin over the small number of votes cast by corporation presidents as opposed to the large number cast by their workers. The writers of such polemics often conclude by "pointing with alarm" at the danger of labor rule in the nation. For whatever comfort it may afford disturbed readers, it should be noted that, at least in the Border States, the wishes of the business community are not ignored. This salutary state of affairs emerges from the very positive correlation between political success and the possession of sufficient economic resources to conduct a vigorous campaign in behalf of the "common man." For example, in the Kentucky Bluegrass very few of the voters own liquor distilleries or horse farms. Still, as Chapter II clearly indicated, the voters of the section have historically evidenced a tender concern for the welfare of those who are so fortunately endowed. The reason for this happy state of affairs in Kentucky is that the Bluegrass political leaders frequently turn to leaders in the horse and liquor world for the wherewithal to conduct political campaigns. The generosity of these gentry to the political leaders does not go unrewarded.

In addition to the political and interest group leaders there is a third group of central importance in political campaigns, i.e., the rank and file members of the major parties. In the chapters dealing with trends, two remarkable aspects of the political behavior of the great bulk of the electorate stand out; 1) the durability of party alignments, and 2) the radical changes in the political environment required for significant enduring change.

People receive their political preconceptions from their parents in the same fashion as all prejudices are transmitted from father to son. A political bias once formed, like a religious affiliation, is difficult to shake. However, about once every generation some earth-shaking event occurs which changes the political environment sufficiently to induce large numbers of people to change their political affiliations. At the same time, however, the political convictions of the great majority of the population remain unaffected. It is this durability of political alignments in company with occasional political change among elements of the population that produces factionalism.

It is no mean task for Border State Democratic leaders to maintain a semblance of unity within a party which contains both Bourbons and New Dealish Negroes. The success of party leaders in their efforts to placate all factions of the party may be measured by the caliber of successful Border State politicians both past and present; men such as Alben Barkley and Earle Clements of Kentucky; Harry Truman of Missouri; Matthew Neely of West Virginia; and Albert C. Ritchie of Maryland.

It is significant that few Border State politicians were prominent on the national stage after the Civil War and before 1932. Seemingly, it is only during periods when the problem of uniting North and South commands national attention that Border State leadership is turned to. Thus just as the Border States produced leaders such as Henry Clay before the Civil War, so after 1932 leaders such as Alben Barkley emerged. These leaders have been trained in the task of holding the North and South together within their own states. Consequently, when the nation faces the same problem they are equipped to mend the wounds and formulate a course of national action which is acceptable to both sections. They are the "great compromisers." But they are also our great unifiers.

SELECTED BIBLIOGRAPHY

BOOKS

AMBLER, CHARLES H. *West Virginia, The Mountain State.* New York: Prentice-Hall, Inc., 1940.

ANDREWS, MATTHEW P. *History of Maryland; Province and State.* Garden City, New York: Doubleday, Doran and Co., Inc., 1929.

BAYLOR, ORVAL. *W. J. Dan Talbott, Champion of Good Government.* Louisville, Kentucky: Kentucky Printing Corp., 1942.

BROWNLOW, LOUIS. *A Passion for Politics, An Autobiography.* Chicago: University of Chicago Press, 1955.

BURT, HENRY J. *The Population of Missouri.* (Agricultural Experiment Station, Research Bulletin 188) Columbia: University of Missouri, 1933.

CLARK, THOMAS D. *A History of Kentucky.* New York: Prentice-Hall, Inc., 1937.

HERR, KINCAID A. *The Louisville and Nashville Railroad, 1850-1942.* Louisville, Kentucky: L & N Magazine, 1943.

KARSCH, ROBERT F. *Essentials of Missouri Government.* Columbia, Missouri: Lucas Bros., 1953.

KEY, V. O., JR. *Politics, Parties, and Pressure Groups.* New York: Thomas Y. Crowell Co., 1950.

MEYERS, WILL S., JR., JOHNSON, JOHN L., MARTIN, JAMES W. *Kentucky Income Payments by Counties 1939, 1947, 1950 and 1951.* (Bureau of Business Research, Bulletin No. 26). Lexington: University of Kentucky, 1953.

MILLIGAN, MAURICE M. *Inside Story of the Pendergast Machine.* New York: Charles Scribners Sons, 1948.

RICHARDSON, PAUL D., BROWN, JAMES. *Population Estimates for Kentucky Counties, April 1, 1953.* (Kentucky Agricultural Experiment Station, Progress Report 14) Lexington: University of Kentucky, 1953.

ST. PATRICK, SISTER MARY. *Political Nativism in the State of Maryland.* Washington, D. C.: The Catholic University of America, 1928.

SHANNON, J. B. *Presidential Politics in Kentucky, 1824-1948.* Lexington: University of Kentucky, 1950.

SNOW, THAD. *From Missouri.* Boston: Houghton Mifflin Co., 1954.

STEFFENS, LINCOLN. *The Shame of the Cities.* New York: Peter Smith, 1948.

TRUMAN, DAVID B. *The Governmental Process.* New York: Alfred A. Knopf, 1951.

WRITERS' PROGRAM. *Maryland, A Guide to the Old Line State.* New York: Oxford University Press, 1940.

WRITERS' PROGRAM. *Missouri, A Guide to the "Show Me" State.* New York: Duell, Sloan and Pearce, 1941.

PUBLIC DOCUMENTS

COMMONWEALTH OF KENTUCKY. *Kentucky Directory,* 1910-1954.

STATE OF MARYLAND. *Maryland Manual,* 1902-1954.

STATE OF MISSOURI. *Official Manual State of Missouri,* 1901-1954.

STATE OF WEST VIRGINIA. *West Virginia Bluebook,* 1916-1954.

U. S. BUREAU OF THE CENSUS. *A Century of Population Growth,* 1790-1900.

——————— *Seventh Census of the United States: 1850. Statistics of the United States.*

——————— *Eighth Census of the United States: 1860. Population.*

——————— *Ninth Census of the United States: 1870. Statistics of the Population.*

——————— *Tenth Census of the United States: 1880. Statistics of the Population, Vol. I.*

——————— *Eleventh Census of the United States: 1890. Report on Population, Part I.*

——————— *Twelfth Census of the United States: 1900. Population, Part I.*

——————— *Thirteenth Census of the United States: 1910. Population, Vols. I and II.*

——————— *Fourteenth Census of the United States: 1920. Population, Vol. II and III.*

——————— *Fifteenth Census of the United States: 1930. Population, Vols. II and III.*

——————— *Sixteenth Census of the United States: 1940. State of Birth of the Native Population.*

———————— *Seventeenth Census of the United States: 1950. Population,* Vol. II.

———————— *Seventeenth Census of the United States: 1950. State of Birth,* Special Report P-E No. 4A.

———————— *Seventeenth Census of the United States: 1950. Nativity and Parentage,* Special Report P-E No. 3A.

ARTICLES AND PERIODICALS

CRISLER, ROBERT M. "Missouri's Little Dixie," *Missouri Historical Review,* XLII (January, 1948), 130-139.

——— ——— "Republican Areas in Missouri," *Missouri Historical Review,* XLII (July, 1948), 299-309.

SAUER, C. O. "Geography and the Gerrymander," *American Political Science Review,* XII (August, 1918), 304-426.

SHANNON, J. B. "Presidential Politics in the South," *Journal of Politics,* I (August, 1939), 278-300.

The Tribune Almanac, 1832-1887.

The World Almanac, 1888-1916.

UNPUBLISHED MATERIAL

BRADSHAW, WILLIAM. "Political Parties in Missouri," Unpublished article, Department of Political Science, University of Missouri.

OLIVER, JOHN. "Study of Kansas City Politics," Unpublished study, Federal Reserve Bank Building, Kansas City, Missouri.

Transcript of Interview of Milton H. Smith, President, Louisville and Nashville Railroad Company, by C. P. Connolly, Representing Hearst Magazines, Louisville, Kentucky, 1913.

OTHER SOURCES

During the course of this study more than one hundred political, farm, labor, and business leaders from Missouri, Kentucky, West Virginia, and Maryland were interviewed. The results of these interviews provided the bulk of the data on which this study is based.

All the figures in this study, except where otherwise indicated, were based upon census data, and election returns contained in the States' Bluebooks and the *Tribune* and *World Almanacs,* save Kentucky's primary returns. In Kentucky it was necessary to obtain the primary returns from the records in the office of the Secretary of State.

INDEX